HOMEMADE
LIQUEURS

HOMEMADE LIQUEURS

DONA AND MEL MEILACH

Contemporary Books, Inc.
Chicago

Library of Congress Cataloging in Publication Data

Meilach, Dona Z
    Homemade liqueurs.

    Bibliography: p.
    Includes index.
    1. Liqueurs.   I. Meilach, Mel, joint author.
II. Title.
TP611.M44   1979   641.8'74   79-13831
ISBN 0-8092-7137-0
ISBN 0-8092-7582-1 pbk.

All photos by Dona and Mel Meilach unless otherwise credited.

Published by Contemporary Books, Inc.
180 North Michigan Avenue, Chicago, Illinois 60601
Manufactured in the United States of America
Library of Congress Catalog Card Number: 79-13831
International Standard Book Number: 0-8092-7137-0 (cloth)
                                    0-8092-7582-1 (paper)

Published simultaneously in Canada by
Beaverbooks, Ltd.
150 Lesmill Road
Don Mills, Ontario M3B 2T5
Canada

Other Books by Dona Z. Meilach

A Modern Approach to Basketry

Contemporary Art with Wood

Contemporary Batik and Ti-Dye

Creating Art with Bread Dough

Decorative and Sculptural Ironwork

Macramé: Creative Design in Knotting

Dona Z. Meilach is the author and co-author of sixty creative books on a variety of subjects. This is the first book she has co-authored with her husband, Mel.

Contents

Foreword

As liqueurs rise in popularity, their consumption increases and interest in them grows accordingly. Just as wine and winemaking developed its followers, so it is with liqueurs. Drinking them, making them, appreciating them can be a fascinating aperitif for further delightful discoveries. Let your investigations thread you back in time to the history of the elixirs in the Middle Ages, perhaps a trip through the monasteries in France and Italy where they are still being made.

It is easy to become caught up in the romance and folklore surrounding herbs and spices. You will undoubtedly discover plants with flavorings you never knew existed. Perhaps you knew the plant existed, but didn't realize its background and use as a flavoring.

Certainly, you will become more knowledgeable about the liqueurs themselves, the tastes, the names, and the variations. With only a little effort you can quickly earn the title of connoisseur, if that is your aim.

Whatever your goal, we hope you will enjoy making the liqueurs, serving and cooking with them as much as we have.

TO YOUR HEALTH!

For Jordan and Adam Seligman

Acknowledgments

Our sincere thanks to the scores of people who put up with us during the preparation of the material for this book.

We are especially grateful to Susan Seligman who helped select, prepare, and test many of the food recipes; to Beverly Stefanski for her individual approach to making many of the liqueur recipes and her double check on some of ours; to Peggy Moulton who ferreted out several recipes from Italian and French farmers and their wives, during an extended stay in Europe. We loved her stories of often severe, but charming, "take it on the chin rebuffs" from commercial distributors from whom she requested "secret" recipes.

Our thanks to our son, Allen Meilach, for the drawings; to Penny McBride and Collette Russell for their help in typing the final manuscript.

We must thank Carol Craford and Norman Brown whose bottles of liqueurs whetted our appetites to make them, too. We wish we could list all our friends who acted as "tasters" at our various parties and/or whenever they walked into our kitchen. We know the recipes are successful because these people are still our friends.

Dona and Mel Meilach
Carlsbad, California 1979

Part 1
Making
Liqueurs

1

A Love Affair with Liqueurs

Opening the pages of this book is like peeping into an endless hall filled with new adventures. Adventures that will expand your taste and smell sensations; adventures into exciting discoveries for fruits, spices, and herbs you use every day; adventures that are waiting for your creative touch, your individual spark to ignite wondrous results.

Making liqueurs and using them in marvelous ways can be all of these if you like to experiment, have fun, and tackle new challenges.

People have made liqueurs, also called cordials, for centuries. As with many other homemade delicacies, industry stepped in and liqueur making became a highly mechanized process. Commercialism promoted the luscious liquids and surrounded them with an aura that they could only be made by highly technical procedures using impossible-to-duplicate secret recipes.

All this is so, with reservations. It is true that industrialized processes cannot be duplicated in the home. Exotic blends using scores of hard-to-find herbs cannot be copied perfectly by the do-it-yourselfer. But excellent simulations of popular and unusual liqueurs can be made—easily—cheaply—legally.

During the past few years, the consumption of soft alcoholic drinks has risen steadily and almost every bottling company in America, France, Italy, Denmark, Holland, Belgium, and elsewhere is scurrying to catch a larger share of the dollar, the mark, the pound, the lira. They are producing an incredible line of new liqueur flavors. Observe the ads in popular magazines if you need convincing. Each year more ads for liqueurs, more flavors, more ideas for using the increasing variety of sweet, delicious elixirs appear.

Perhaps the greatest impetus for today's increased liqueur usage began a few years ago when companies producing Grand Marnier, Sabra, Amaretto, and other flavors promoted their products for use in the kitchen for cooking. They distributed beautifully illustrated booklets with a variety of irresistible recipes. Until then, liqueurs, because of their sweetness, were associated with desserts and mixed drinks. Soon, cooks everywhere, from simple kitchens to banquet facilities, were awakened to the flavoring potential of liqueurs added to appetizers, entrées, breads, salads, and soups.

The costs of research, advertising, and marketing full color recipe booklets are all built into the cost of the product; the price of a bottle of liqueur reflects these costs in addition to the ingredients and the profit margins. Today, a fifth of a popular brand liqueur of an unusual flavor may cost $10 to $15 per bottle; lesser known brands of usual flavors run in the $4 to $10 range. If you make your own liqueurs in the same quantities the cost is closer to $1.50 to $2 per bottle.

DEFINITIONS

Before we proceed, we should define "liqueur" and the words associated with it. "Liqueur" is derived from the Latin word *liquefacere* which means "to dissolve." A liqueur is made by dissolving a flavor in alcohol which is then sweetened.

"Cordial" is used interchangeably with "liqueur" in popular parlance. At one time it is believed the word cordial referred to fruit drinks flavored with brandy but research on this is hazy.

"Ratafia" is also synonymous with liqueur and cordial. Its origin is interesting and believed to have been derived from the custom of drinking a toast when a treaty was ratified, according to the historical book, *Brandies and Liqueurs of the World.*

"Eau de vie" is a generic term for spirits made of fruits and alcohol that have been distilled with no sweetener added.

Fruit brandy is a distilled dry spirit made from the fermented mash of fruits. To avoid confusion, note that most liqueurs are *flavored* with the fruit essence; while all fruit brandies *are* the fruit essence.

PRODUCTION PROCESSES

It is essential to understand the basic processes involved in making liqueurs: *distillating* and *macerating*. *Distillating* is the process of manufacturing alcoholic beverages using fermenting and distillation procedures. Whiskey is distilled from fermented "mash" made of corn, rye, wheat, malt, and other small grains and water. Brandy is made from the fermented juice of grapes and other fruits. Rum is made from fermented molasses and sugar cane juice.

Distillation employs heat that extracts gas or vapor from the liquid to remove any impurities. When the necessary impurities are removed, and the liquid is "rectified," pure alcohol results.

Macerating, the process most often used to make liqueurs, is essentially the same as "steeping," the word we use throughout the book. Macerating, or steeping, to make liqueur can be compared to making tea. A flavoring substance such as soft fruits, herbs, spices, nuts, beans, and so forth, is placed in alcohol, usually vodka, brandy, or whiskey. The flavoring is absorbed by the alcohol over a short steeping period of about one to three weeks and then the flavoring substance is strained or filtered out. Sweetener is added to result in the finished liqueur which is allowed to mature, perhaps two weeks to several months to enhance the bouquet and the flavor.

ADVANTAGES OF MAKING LIQUEURS

Why make your own liqueurs? We have already pointed out the cost factor. If you require further convincing, price a bottle of a brand name Amaretto, Curaçao, or coffee liqueur; divide the number of ounces in the bottle by the cost to arrive at the cost per ounce. Compare this with the cost per ounce of inexpensive vodka. A fifth of liqueur, 25.6 ounces, requires approximately 16 ounces of vodka plus the flavoring and one-half cup of sugar, all minimal costs.

Saving money is only one reason to make liqueurs. You can alter the flavors, make them stronger or weaker, sweeter or drier. You can combine flavors according to your taste preferences and build up an incredible variety of flavors for sipping and for cooking.

Serving liqueurs you make yourself to guests always leads to sparkling conversation. You'll enjoy the curious expression when someone tastes a drink, a sauce, or soup with a hard to pinpoint flavor, and asks: "What ever did you put into it?" You will become very knowledgeable about essences, concentrates and other factors.

Liqueur making can be gallons of fun. Steeping an in-season fruit in vodka, turning the bottle every few days, is like nursing along your own creation. You filter it, taste it, sweeten it, and age it. That waiting period can seem interminable, even if it's only a few weeks. When you uncap the bottle and taste it, it is an achievement. It doesn't matter whether it is delicious on the first try or needs a little something more. Each mixture is a discovery, and you'll feel like a chemist waiting to see what the new ingredients in the test tube have hatched.

TASTING PARTIES

Liqueur-tasting parties are a bonus. While preparing and testing our own mixes for this book, we hesitated to offer recipes using only our biased viewpoints. We

held several "tasting" parties. Each group tested six different flavors; the limit most people could effectively judge in one evening. Liqueurs were poured in clear sight of the judges from attractive bottles, all with coded labels. If you pour them where the judges cannot see the bottle, it does not matter.

For the first parties we used traditional one- and two-ounce stemmed cordial glasses with only enough liqueur in each glass for people to look at the color, inhale the bouquet, and sip the liqueur. Nuts and crackers were nibbled between each sample to eliminate any lingering flavor from a previous taste. In addition to the color, bouquet, and taste, we asked people to comment on the following:

- smoothness of the drink
- strength of the flavor
- if the spices were subtle or overpowering
- how close the beverage tasted to the commercial flavor
- any other characteristics

We always followed the "official six tasted flavors" with commercial counterparts. In all fairness, we admit that the commercial Benedictine and chocolates were always voted superior to ours. But our fruit drinks, such as pineapple, orange, plum, prune, cassis, banana,

cherry, the nut flavors, and many of the herb and spice liqueurs were rated very high in comparison and often preferable to the commercial varieties because they were not as sweet and thick.

Experience taught us to serve the first few samples in the stemmed cordial glasses for effect but, because of the number needed and the washing problem, we used disposable plastic one-ounce cups available at medical supply houses (physicians use them for dispensing medicines).

It is essential to emphasize the visual-psychological aspect of homemade liqueurs. Serve them in carefully labeled pretty bottles or decanters and they will "taste" better than the same mix served from a crudely labeled and corked beer bottle. We experimented several times by serving the same homemade liqueur in both kinds of bottles poured in full view of the sipper. In every instance, the drink poured from the pretty bottle was judged better. We duplicated the procedure with commercial liqueurs; always the one poured from the pretty bottle was judged superior though both were the same. So much for taste-testing.

HOW LIQUEURS CAME TO BE

We often wondered how the monks in the ancient monasteries arrived at the final results of their testing. Hippocrates in the fifth century B.C. is believed to have been the first man to flavor alcohol with herbs and aromatic plants, but his brew is described as "fit only for the strongest men."

Elixirs as "digestifs," or aids to digestion and stomach distress, evolved in the Middle Ages. Alchemists of the thirteenth century were seeking preventives and cures for the dread diseases of the time. By heating alcohol, they drove the gas or vapor from it to result, not in a cureall, but in a condensed alcoholic beverage triple the strength of the original, thus giving rise to distilled spirits. Spices and fruits were added to these drinks to make them somewhat palatable.

In that dawning age of science, the alchemists were not taken seriously. The monks were among the few literate people of the time and they were able to experiment with formulae gleaned from alchemists and ancient records. So, the monasteries assumed the task of making liqueurs and their findings were acceptable. The religious orders had the money to buy the rare herbs and spices that were beginning to arrive via new trade routes from other countries.

The early blends made by the monks were harsh. The introduction of sugar cane from the New World by Columbus brought about the sweetening of these early elixirs and led to the eventual assortment of liqueurs similar to those we know today.

Best known and among the oldest liqueurs were those made by the Benedictine monks at Fécamp Abbey, France. The original recipe contains twenty-seven different herbs and dried plants including Ceylon tea, juniper berries, balm, angelica, cinnamon, cloves, nutmeg, vanilla, and more. It is thought to have been compounded about 1510 by the monk Dom Bernardo Vincelli but during the vicissitudes of France, its wars, and so forth, the recipe was lost. Benedictine is still bottled in France by descendants of Alexander Le Grand who, in 1863, found a recipe he believed to be very close to the original formula and began to produce it commercially.

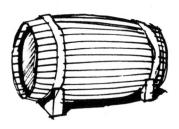

Le Grand built an ornate, Renaissance style palace at
Fécamp in 1876, according to historians Hurst Hannum
and Robert Blumberg. Here are housed the Benedictine
distillery and aging cellars as well as a museum which is
open to the public.

There are other liqueur-producing monasteries open
to the public. In Italy, near Florence, one can fan out in
various directions and find them. Monte Senario is to
the north of the city, Vallombrosa to the east, and
Certosa to the south. They all maintain pharmacias, or
bars, where small bottles of their blends may be tasted
and purchased at very nominal costs. Any liqueur
aficionado could easily plan a trip through France and
Italy taking in the liqueur-producing spots in the same
way one would plan a trip through Northern California's Napa Valley for a wine-tasting tour.

ABOUT SERVING LIQUEURS

Traditionally, liqueurs have been served in one- to two-
ounce gracefully shaped, delicate, stemmed glasses and
this continues to be popular. However, the increased
use of the aromatic drinks has changed any strict right
or wrong concepts about service. Today we are free to
do our own thing and serve them any way we like.
Tulip-shaped glasses and balloon-shaped brandy snifters
channel the scents directly to the nostrils and, though
such glasses hold four to six ounces, there is nothing
wrong with placing only a small amount in the glass.
We have served liqueurs in Japanese sake cups, in wine
glasses, on the rocks, and straight up. Anything is cor-
rect.

A special glass is marketed for serving a "frappé," a
drink made by pouring liqueur over a heaped mound of
crushed ice. A wine or champagne glass is equally as
serviceable as the frappé glass.

The temperature at which a drink is served has also

been written about in many books. Most suggest serving them at room temperature, but chilling some liqueurs can enhance the taste. Chill the glass or place the bottle in a freezer for a short time before serving to create an elegant taste sensation. Many flavors taste delicious served over ice but this does dilute them.

Some spice and herb liqueurs have a more pronounced aroma and taste when they are slightly warm. Never boil a liqueur or the alcohol will evaporate. Use a brandy warmer, or place the glass in a dish of hot water for a few minutes to warm it through, or in a microwave oven for a few seconds.

Use the liqueurs you make to impart flavor and smoothness to scores of mixed drinks. Several of the more popular recipes are given beginning on page 132. Consult bar guide books for additional combinations and invent some of your own.

Liqueurs have also traditionally been served before dinner as aperitifs and after dinner as digestifs, depending upon the base flavor. Now even the "when" of liqueur service is flexible. The flavors are delicious by themselves, and in mixed drinks before or after any meal of the day and any time in-between. For cooking, they are welcome additions to recipes used for breakfast, lunch, dinner, and snacks. Try a sip or two of your favorite liqueur as a nightcap. An ounce or two is less alcoholic and caloric than a full glass of Scotch or bourbon, and equally as warming and relaxing.

Recipes presented throughout the book for making liqueurs, and the foods and drinks using them, have been tested and are offered in good faith. Many varying factors of some basic ingredients will affect the final product. Fruit, for example, varies in ripeness, size, and origin. The water used and the freshness of other ingredients are all elusive qualities that can cause different results using the same quantities and ratios indicated. Tastes also vary. We have made every effort to standardize amounts and equivalents but it must be emphasized that the authors, publisher, and any other agency that has cooperated in the preparation of this book cannot be held responsible for the results.

2

Liqueur Basics

The ingredients and equipment you need to make liqueurs are easily available and very uncomplicated. The procedure might be compared to making tea: Flavoring (tea leaves) is added to a base liquid (water) and allowed to steep. In liqueur making, the steeping process is referred to as "macerating": A flavoring material is steeped in an alcohol base such as vodka or brandy and a sweetener is added. If you have flavoring materials in your kitchen and vodka in your bar, you can easily make a liqueur which can be ready for consumption in a few days. Most flavoring ingredients are as close as your grocery, health-food, and gourmet-cooking stores.

Basically, you need:

INGREDIENTS

Flavorings: Fresh or dried fruits, fresh and dried herbs, spices, nuts, beans, whole fruits, peels, pulp, seeds, roots, flowers, and leaves are used.

Extracts used for baking are chocolate, mint, almond, vanilla, peppermint, etc. Always buy pure extracts, not imitation flavorings.

Concentrates sold specifically for making liqueurs in wine-making shops, Italian food markets, and gourmet shops are used. "Noirot" and "Creative Cordial" are reliable and available brands.

Alcohol base

Vodka (80 proof or higher when available). Also brandy, rum, gin, whiskey, or neutral spirits.

Sweetening

A sugar syrup made of two parts sugar and one part water is boiled together for about five minutes until the sugar dissolves. It is then cooled and added to the flavored alcohol.

Mild-flavored honey such as orange or clover honey.

To Make Sugar Syrup

1 cup white
granulated sugar ⎱ 1 cup sugar
½ cup water   ⎰ syrup

Boil together until sugar dissolves.

Optional

Smoothers or thickeners. Glycerine from the drugstore or prepared smoothers make the product feel thicker or heavier to the taste. Use about one teaspoon per quart.

Coloring. Any prepared or natural food coloring. A prepared food coloring, usually yellow or green (avoid red), or a natural food colorant: saffron, spinach, watercress.

EQUIPMENT

Glass bottles with covers (DO NOT USE PLASTICS):

1. Wide-mouth gallon and quart jars for mixing and steeping. Save empty jars from food products such as soups, jellies, salad dressings (with lids), or use canning jars.
2. Jars for aging can have narrow necks. For small recipes or dividing large recipes into two bottles, we like the dark bottles from beer. Always wash and

sterilize used bottles in a dishwasher or by pouring boiling water into them to remove any residue from previous ingredients.

3. Decorative bottles for serving or gift giving. Save decanters and bottles from commercial liqueurs, liquors, and wines.
4. Measuring cups, measuring spoons.
5. Small kitchen diet scale with measurements by ounce and gram.
6. Filter materials of diminishing coarseness: wire strainers, cheesecloth, unbleached muslin, coffee filters, chemists' filters.
7. Funnel, corks, waxed paper, or paraffin wax for sealing.
8. Fun items: Decorative corks, sealing tubes, personalized labels.

PROCEDURES

Briefly, there are two basic approaches for making liqueurs at home:

1. By steeping, or macerating, the flavoring of fruit, herb, etc., in alcohol. The mix is allowed to steep for several days, weeks, or months. During this steeping period, the mixture is turned or shaken a few times a week. It is then strained and filtered. The sweetener is added to result in the clear, tasty finished liqueur. An aging or maturing period that helps to develop the full bouquet and flavor may require a few days or several months. Except when otherwise specified, the liqueurs presented in this book should be matured several weeks or months. Taste is the real test.

2. Adding flavored non-alcoholic concentrates to sugar syrup and alcohol. All are prepared the same way, following specific label directions. "Noirot" is one brand that is reliable and that has been marketed for several years, but there are other brands on the market. You'll find them in wine-making and gourmet shops. Use a one-quart bottle and:

   a. Pour *two* cups sugar syrup (made by boiling *two* cups sugar and *one* cup water) into a clean, empty one-quart bottle. (Adjust the sweetness by reducing or increasing the amount of syrup.)

   b. Add the concentrate.

   c. Fill the bottle with vodka.

Steeping, or macerating fresh fruits in vodka requires only the fruits, the vodka, and flavorings. Sweetener may be added after the steeping period.

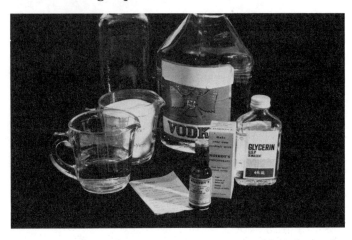

Concentrates are pre-flavored; they are poured into the vodka with the sweetener. They are ready to drink after about 24 hours . . . enough time to permit all the ingredients to blend.

NOTE: To make one quart of liqueur, you will always use less than a quart of vodka (closer to three cups) as the sugar syrup and flavorings constitute some of the volume.

The best way to understand how to make a liqueur is to do it. Most recipes yield a quart (32 ounces) or ⅘ quart (25.6 oz.) of each liqueur. We have found it wise to make many flavors in smaller quantities, yielding about 2 cups (16 oz.) to 3 cups (24 oz.) of finished liqueur, depending upon the amount of sugar syrup added. This allows you to test a recipe and to experiment with portions of it for sweetening and adding smoothers. When you make several flavors, large quantities become costly due to the amount of vodka required. The number of large bottles and space to store them can also be a problem. Dark beer bottles are easy to come by and hold about 1¾ cups. They are excellent for storing and aging. Before serving or giving your mixes for gifts, transfer the liqueurs into decorative decanters or bottles.

In January 1979, the American wine industry switched all bottles to metric measurements. The following should help you sort out liquid measures and bottle sizes. It is sobering to note that in making homemade liqueurs, the exact ratio of flavorings to sugar syrup to alcohol is not critical.

1 Gallon = 64 Ounces
1.75 Liters = 59.2 Ounces
1.5 Liters = 50.7 Ounces
2/5 Gallon = 51.2 Ounces
1 Liter = 33.8 Ounces
1 Quart = 32 Ounces
750 Milliliters = 25.4 Ounces
4/5 Quart (One 5th) = 25.6 Ounces
2 Cups = 1 Pint = 16 Ounces = ½ Quart
4/5 Pint = 12.8 Ounces
375 Milliliters = 12.7 Ounces
¼ Liter = 8.5 Ounces
1 Cup = 8 Ounces
100 Milliliters = 3.4 Ounces
1 Jigger = 1½ Ounces
1 Tablespoon = ½ Ounce or 3 Teaspoons
1 Dash = 3 Drops or 1/32 Ounce
1 Millileter = 1/5 Teaspoon

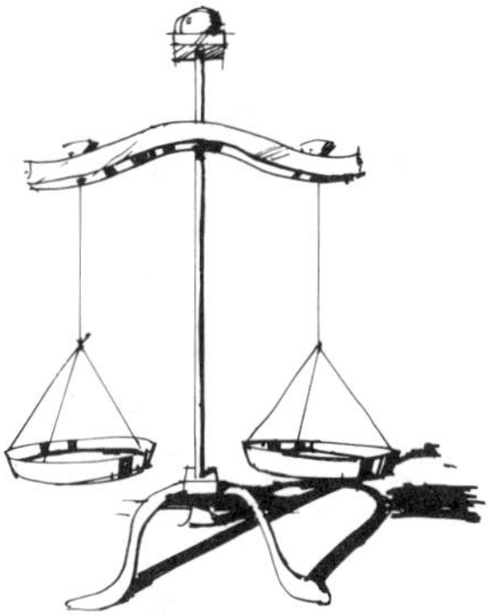

For additional weights and measure charts and conversion tables, please refer to the Appendix.

About the alcohol base

Liqueurs derive their character from the flavorings used, not from the alcohol base. Therefore, a flavorless base is most desirable, and vodka fills that requirement. Use the least expensive charcoal-filtered (it removes impurities) vodka you can find and purchase it in large-size bottles for greatest economy.

Most vodka in the U.S. today is 80 proof and ideal for making liqueurs. Proof refers to a mixture of alcohol and water containing a standard of alcohol of a specific gravity (0.7939) at 60°. In U.S. measure, this means the alcohol is double the percent in volume of the water. A 200 proof is pure alcohol. 100 proof means the mixture is 50/50 alcohol and water. Thus an 80-proof beverage would contain 40 percent alcohol and 60 percent water.

The addition of sugar syrup increases the ratio of water, thereby cutting the proof of the vodka. One cup of sugar syrup added to three cups of 80-proof vodka dilutes the alcohol to yield a 60-proof liqueur. When two cups of sugar syrup are added to three cups of 80-proof vodka, a 48-proof liqueur results (approximately).

Grain neutral spirits may be available in larger liquor stores in some areas. It is 190-proof and should be diluted half and half with water.

Brandy (80 proof) will blend well with a variety of fruit and herb flavors. Cherry brandy and apricot brandy recipes given are made by steeping the fruit in unflavored brandy instead of vodka; often a combination of vodka and brandy will result in an entirely different taste for the finished product.

Rum can be used for citrus flavors and for many berries. Whiskey and gin usually have their own individual flavors so must be used with discretion. They are the basis of Irish Mist, Drambuie, and Cutty Sark. Certainly, experiment with them in small quantities to create your own mixtures.

About flavorings

The first half of this book is all about the flavorings adaptable to liqueur making: fresh and dried fruits, fresh and dried spices, herbs, leaves, beans, and others. Each will be described in accompanying recipes. Unusual ingredients or those you may not be familiar with can be found in gourmet food shops, health food stores, or by mail order from the sources listed in the Appendix. Almost all fruit and nut flavorings that are strained out of the steeped alcohol mix may be used to create a "Fruitueur's Fantasy" and added to foods as the mood moves you:

Fruitueur's fantasy

Use a large, dark glass jar or crockery pot with a tight-fitting cover. When you strain fruits from mixes, add them to one another in the jar. With each addition, place about ¼ cup sugar into the jar along with about ⅛ cup vodka or brandy (or just enough to cover the fruits). Store in the refrigerator or at a cool (not over 45° F.) temperature to prevent fermentation. Stir with every addition. Fresh fruits may be added such as berries, peeled sliced peaches, apricots, and pineapple. (Do NOT use herbs and spices with strong flavors which would overpower the fruits.) Serve as a condiment with meat dishes. Use it in cakes, puddings, pies, over ice cream, in parfaits. It will last indefinitely so long as you continue adding to it.

About sweeteners

A "liqueur," by definition, is a sweetened spirit flavored by a vegetable substance. The amount of sweetness in a liqueur can vary according to taste: Commercial liqueurs are almost always quite sweet—sometimes too sweet. Reducing the sweetness to taste is one of the bonuses of making your own. A very sweet liqueur is usually termed a "crème," such as Crème de Cassis or Crème de Menthe. A crème must contain at least 400 grams of sugar per liter (40%) in commercial production. A minimum sugar content of 200 grams is designated for French-made liqueurs (20%).

We suggest using a ratio of one cup of sugar syrup (8 oz.) to three cups (24 oz.) alcohol and adjusting more or less to taste. In most recipes, though not all, the sweetener is added after the flavoring and alcohol have steeped. To taste test, place two tablespoons of the mixture in a small cup with two tablespoons of sugar syrup. Taste. If it is too strong, dilute by adding one more tablespoon of the liqueur at a time. If not sweet enough, add more sugar syrup. Aim for something like two parts liqueur to one part sweetener, 3 to 1, or 4 to 1, etc. Always record your additions carefully, then transpose to the full recipe.

Sugar syrup is usually used for the addition as dry sugar does not dissolve easily in alcohol.

For medium sweetening, use one cup sugar syrup. Here's the recipe for Sugar Syrup #1:

| 1 cup *white granulated sugar* | } | 1 cup sugar |
| ½ cup water | | syrup |

Bring to a boil, and stir until all the sugar is dissolved and the mixture is clear. Always cool before adding to alcohol mixture; heat causes alcohol to evaporate. If tap water is heavily chlorinated or bad tasting, heat the syrup a few minutes to drive off chlorination. Distilled water may be used.

For sweeter mixtures, use two cups of sugar syrup (made by doubling above recipe).

Raw sugar and brown sugar may be used to vary the taste. Try Sugar Syrup #2:

¾ cup brown sugar (light or dark)⎫
½ cup granulated white sugar   ⎬ 1 cup sugar
½ cup water   ⎭ syrup

Boil and dissolve as above.

A *mild-flavored honey* may also be used; honey tends to cloud the liqueur, however. When honey is used, the mixture should be allowed to sit undisturbed for a few weeks; then the clear top solution is siphoned off. The remaining bottom portion can be used for cooking or added to the "Fruitueurs's Fantasy" (page 23).

If using honey: substitute 1 to 1¼ cup of honey for 1 cup sugar syrup.

About smoothers

Glycerine is used by commercial liqueur makers to give the product a feeling of "thickness" so it rolls on your tongue as you taste it. It is sold as a proprietary item on your druggist's shelf. It is the same glycerine used to make the well-known soothing non-chap solution of glycerine and rosewater. Wine-supply companies also market a prepared smoothing product composed of glycerol and sorbital. The addition of glycerine is optional; it does not affect the taste. It provides taste texture and adds a psychological effect.

Add about 1 teaspoon glycerine or prepared smoother per quart of finished liqueur.

EXPERIMENT: Add ¼ teaspoon glycerine to 1 cup finished liqueur. Shake well and bottle. Bottle another cup without glycerine. Age for a week or two; compare tastes and textures.

About coloring

Many liqueurs are clear or light-colored amber and subtle earth shades depending upon the flavoring. To color liqueurs add any pure food coloring sold for cooking and baking. The visual-taste sensation will have greater impact if a touch of yellow is added to banana, pink to cherry, green to mint. Use liquid or paste coloring very sparingly. Mix tiny droplets into a small amount of the liqueur, then add the colored portion to the whole recipe until you achieve the shade desired.

Purists may prefer natural substances for coloring: a pinch of saffron in the steeping mix will turn it a beautiful yellow.

For a green color, use a small amount of fresh spinach leaves, parsley, or watercress. Place in blender along with a small amount of water; use the finest grind on the blender. Add a drop or two of the resulting colored water to the alcohol mix. You don't want to add much flavor.

About filtering

Following the suggested steeping time, the solids used for flavoring must be separated from the liquid through a filtering process. The liquid is poured off through three or four filtering materials beginning with a strainer or cheesecloth and graduating to muslin and finally a coarse or fine-grain paper filter. Paper filters are available from grocery stores as coffee filters or from chemists or pharmacies. Use a rubber band to secure the filter cloth over a wide-mouth jar or support the cloth in a funnel and pour the liquid through. Pour any bottom residue into the filter cloth, grasp the filter at the top, and twist it until all the liquid is squeezed through.

When filtering, place the jar in a flat glass baking dish or pan; if you spill any of the liquid, you can retrieve it. As the filter material clogs, move it about or replace it as necessary. Discard or wash used cheesecloth and muslin so as not to transfer flavors from one liqueur to another.

After filtering, measure the remaining amount of liquid since some is lost through spillage and evaporation. This is the time to add sweetening to taste or by the prescribed ratio of three cups flavored alcohol to one cup sweetener. The flavor may change after the liqueur has matured for a few weeks, so additional sweetening may be added at that time.

Eliminating cloudiness

Cloudiness will not hurt a liqueur; it affects only its visual quality. Cloudy portions may be used for drinking or in cooking. To eliminate cloudiness, allow the sediment to settle at the bottom for a few days. Carefully pour the top clear liquid into another bottle so only the sediment remains in the initial bottle. If this procedure is not successful, the clear liquid may be separated from the sediment by siphoning.

Siphoning

Siphoning is used to carry a liquid from a higher level to a lower level by way of a rubber or plastic tube. We suggest a tube about two feet long with one end bent and inserted into the full bottle of liqueur to within about half an inch of the sediment.

Place a second, empty bottle below the full bottle:

The neck of the empty bottle must be about even with the bottom of the full bottle. Suck on the free end of the tube until it fills with the liqueur; quickly place your finger over the end (to prevent spillage), then remove your finger and instantly insert the end into the empty bottle. The liquid from the top bottle will flow into the bottom one.

The principle of siphoning is based on air pressure on the surface of liquid in the top bottle. When you want the flow to stop, raise the bottom bottle so that the top of the liquid now in it will be about equal to or higher than the sediment remaining in the top bottle.

Beer-making companies market special corks with holes in them to secure the siphon tube. Ready-made siphon tubes are available which can be adapted to liqueur making.

A few more guidelines

Always use very clean glass jars. Never use plastic bottles or even plastic-lined lids as the flavor of the plastic permeates liqueurs. Glass jars should be rinsed with very hot water or put through a dishwasher a couple of times to eliminate any trace of previous usage. Wide-mouth jars are convenient for adding and removing fruit and flavorings when you mix, steep, and filter; they also help minimize loss of precious ingredients. For storing, narrow neck jars are fine. Dark jars are preferred; but when they are not available, secure a piece of black construction paper around any jar with a tape or rubber band. Store the jars in a relatively dark place at room temperature wherever you have space.

Finished liqueurs can be aged or matured a minimum of one week in previously used dark liqueur bottles, beer bottles, and so forth. It is impossible to dictate an exact maturation period or to determine shelf life of

homemade liqueurs. We have noticed that orange liqueurs improve with standing, but other flavors have lost some of their punch after about eight months. The solution is to serve—and enjoy—them.

Seal the bottle well at every stage to prevent evaporation. Use corks or screw-on metal lids with a layer of waxed paper under the cork or lid to help keep the jar airtight. Jars may be sealed with a layer of paraffin wax. Bottle seals may be used; they are tubes of a special material that are soaked in warm water and placed over the cork and bottle neck. When dry, the tube shrinks tightly around the bottle and cork and seals them.

About labels and records

Once you get into the spirit of making liqueurs, make life easier by forming a habit of using labels to record the recipes and the progress. It's so easy to forget ingredients, dates for filtering, and so on. Use color-coded labels and you'll be in production before you know it. We suggest self-sticking labels from stationery stores.

1. Use a large white label on the bottle to indicate the ingredients, amounts, and date made. Also notate the date to filter. Later, remove this label from the bottle and transfer to a notebook or file card and file box with additional information including filtering dates, amount of sweetener added, your comments about taste. If you want to duplicate the recipe, you can; if you want to change it, you know where the alterations can be made.
2. Use green labels to indicate those bottles that need to be filtered; the projected filtering date should be noted on them.
3. Blue labels can indicate bottles that are finished with the aging time and the projected "finished" date noted. You can also include your taste test dates and comments. The white label is removed and filed when the liqueur is finished.
4. Decorative, personalized labels are fun to place on finished bottles, and they make your product look professional. You can buy them ready-made with a space for any title you like. For gift giving, add lettering with press-on letters sold in art and stationery supply stores.

Work out your own system, but do record everything.

Liqueur reference list

Many brands of liqueurs that have been produced for generations—sometimes centuries—have become almost synonymous with their flavors. The best known cherry-flavored liqueur is Cherry Heering or Peter Heering. "Heering's Cherry Brandy" was developed in 1818 from an old recipe using red cherries of southern Denmark and distributed by the Heering Trading Company. Benedictine, originally produced by monks of the Benedictine order at Fécamp Abbey, France, is made of a blend of about 50 herbs; it is now made commercially by a firm in France. Kahlua, a popular Mexican coffee liqueur, has become the name used when referring to almost any coffee liqueur although there are other coffee brands on the market. Grand Marnier and Curaçao have become almost common names for any orange liqueurs though in reality they differ in their taste and recipes. Grand Marnier's distinguishing characteristic is that it has cognac as its alcohol base.

It is unlawful to make liqueurs and call them by their trade names. It is also impossible to duplicate specific brands as they are made under highly guarded secret recipes and conditions. But it is entirely possible to simulate flavors in the liqueurs you make and to use them for drinking, cooking, and gift giving. You might discover that your facsimiles are as good as, perhaps better than, the commercial varieties and certainly will cost you less.

As you peruse displays in liquor stores, you will undoubtedly discover more. Every year, new flavors become the "in" liqueurs for the season. Often a company will market a combination of flavors; for example Pistachia first appeared a couple of years ago made essentially from pistachio nuts and spices. When Jimmy Carter was elected President, a peanut liqueur appeared on the market which we quickly made from our own recipe based on experience and common sense.

The following list will help you to identify basic flavorings of the various liqueurs:

Liqueur	*Flavoring*	*Concentrates available*
Absinthe	Herbs, wormwood	
Advocaat	Egg yolks	
Amaretto	Apricot pits & almond	Amaretto
Angelica	Angelica & spices	
Anisette	Anise seed	Anisette green/white
Apricot	Apricot	Apricot
Aquavit	Caraway seeds	
Banana	Banana	
B&B™ or Benedictine & Brandy	Herbs—angelica	Reverendine
Benedictine™	Herbs—angelica	Reverendine
Bitters	Herbs and fruits	
Blackberry	Blackberry	Blackberry
Black Tea	Tea & spices	
Calvados	Fermented apple juice	
Carlsberg	Herbs & mineral water	
Carmella	Caramel & vanilla	
Cassis	Black currant	Black currant
Cerasella	Cherry	
Chartreuse™ Green	Spices & herbs	Green Convent
Chartreuse™ Yellow	Spices & herbs	White Convent
Cherry Blossom	Cherry blossoms	
Cherry	Cherry	Cherry brandy
Cherry Heering	Cherry	
Cherry Marnier	Cherry	
Cherry Suisse	Chocolate & cherry	
Chocolate	Chocolate & vanilla	
Coconut	Coconut	
CocoRibe™	Coconut	
Coffee	Coffee	Moka
Cointreau™	Oranges & brandy	
Cranberry	Cranberry	
Crème d'Ananas	Pineapple-brandy & vanilla	

Liqueur	Flavoring	Concentrates available
Crème de Banana	Banana	Banana
Crème de Cacao	Cacao beans & vanilla	Cocoa
Crème de Café	Coffee	
Crème de Cassis	Black currants	Black currant
Crème de Cerise	Sweet cherries	
Crème de Cumin	Kümmel (caraway)	Kümmel
Crème de Fraises	Strawberry	
Crème de Framboise	Raspberry	Raspberry
Crème de Menthe	Peppermint	Green mint
Crème de Moka	Coffee beans & brandy	
Crème de Noix	Walnuts	
Crème de Noisette	Hazelnuts	
Crème de Noyau	Peach & apricot kernels	Sweet almond
Crème de Prunelle	Plums & prunes	Peach, prunella, pear
Crème de Poire	Pear	Pear
Crème de Recco	Tea leaves & brandy	
Crème de Roses	Rose petals & vanilla	
Crème de Vanille	Vanilla	Vanilla
Crème de Violets	Violet petals	
Crème de Yvette™	Violet petals	
Cuervo Almondrado	Tequila (cactus sap) & almonds	
Curaçao	Green orange peels	Orange red Curaçao
Cutty Sark™	Sweetened whiskey	
Danziger	Orange peels	Lorbuis, Danzig
Drambuie	Herbs, honey, whiskey	Lorbuis
Forbidden Fruit	Grapefruit, brandy, oranges	
Galliano™	Herbs & spices	Yellow Genepy
Goldwasser	Lemon or orange peel, spices	Yellow Genepy
Grand Marnier™	Orange	Orange brandy
Irish Mist	Herbs, Irish whiskey, honey	
Kahlua™	Coffee	Moka
Kirsch or Kirschwasser	Fermented cherries & brandy	Kirsch

Liqueur	Flavoring	Concentrates available
Kümmel	Caraway seeds	Kümmel
Mandarine	Mandarin oranges or tangerines	Tangerine
Maraschino	Maraschino cherries	Maraschino
Millefiori	Flower petals & plants	Floraues
O Cha	Green tea	
Ouzo	Anise	
Parfait amour	Lemon peel & vanilla	
Papaya	Sometimes flower petals	
Peach	Peaches	
Peanut	Peanuts	
Peppermint	Peppermint	White mint
Pernod	Anise	
Peter Heering™	Cherries	
Pineapple	Pineapple	
Pistachia	Pistachio nuts	
Plum	Plums	
Prunelle	Plums & prunes	
Quince	Quince	
Rosemary	Herbs	
Sabra™	Orange & chocolate	
Sambuco™	Licorice & herbs	
Slivovitz	Plum	
Sloe Gin	Sloe berries	Sloe Gin
Southern Comfort™	Peaches, oranges, bourbon	
Strega™	Herbs & spices	Stress
Tequila™	Cactus juices	
Tia Maria™	Coffee	Café Sport
Triple Sec (Cointreau™)	Oranges	
Van der Hum™	Tangerine	
Vandermint™	Chocolate & mint	
Wishniak	Cherry	

NOTE: ™ is the abbreviation for "trademark."

3

Citrus Fruit Liqueurs

Making liqueurs from fresh citrus fruits during their most bountiful growing season is a great satisfaction. You are using nature's ingredients. You can enjoy the results all year around. Citrus fruits are almost always available. Try oranges, lemons, limes, grapefruit, and combinations of them. They are popular as drinks, and your guests will think you're an absolute genius when you serve your own mix of curaçao or triple sec.

We offer basic recipes for whole fruits, peels, and juices with ideas for adding ingredients so you can be as creative as you dare with the tastes. Once you familiarize yourself with the procedures, you'll realize there is no mystery. "Secret" recipes—hoarded by companies and farmers who compete with one another in Italy and France for the "best" liqueur—have found their blends the same way you will: by experimenting through trial-and-error.

Except there's no way to make a mistake. If one liqueur is too sweet, add a bit of lemon to it and re-steep. If it's too sour or bitter, add more sweetener. If the flavor is too weak, add more of the flavoring and repeat the steeping process or add ¼ teaspoon of the necessary pure extract.

To enhance a basic flavor, add another flavor: a pinch of coriander, cinnamon, almond, caraway, or lime peel either to the original blend or after you have steeped and tasted the liqueur.

After your initial successes, you will quickly graduate to creating combinations of fruits such as orange and pear or orange and currants. Take a cue and inspiration from commercial varieties and combine fruits with herbs, nuts, and so forth for such concoctions as orange with chocolate, coconut, or cherry.

The inherent flavor of fruits can be unpredictable. They differ by type, where grown, the season, and sweetness. Before sweetening, use the taste test (Chapter 2), adding the sweetener tablespoon-by-tablespoon until a ratio is established. Remember, the greater the amount of sugar syrup added, the lower the alcoholic content. This permits you to adjust the alcohol and flavor to create a tangy, piquant after-dinner drink, or a sweeter liqueur to mix into a variety of recipes. Strained citrus peels may be used to make candied fruits (See recipe, page 183.)

We also suggest mixing an "eau de vie," an alcoholic beverage made from flavoring and alcohol but NOT sweetened. It may serve as an addition to other liqueurs that need an extra touch of flavor. Simply set aside some of the flavored steeped mixes in bottles after filtering but without sweetening. Some eaux de vie are commercially bottled and available, should you want to keep them on your shelf to add to your own mixes.

After sweetening, allow the liqueur to mature at least a week before drinking; a month is better if your patience will permit. Storage periods tend to round out taste, flavor, and brilliance and to allow the ingredients to interact, resulting in a bouquet and flavor characteristic of a good product. Liqueurs sweetened with honey will be cloudy. After maturing, the clear portion may be siphoned off as described on pages 27-29. The cloudy portion may be saved and used in cooking.

Pure orange extracts and concentrates may be substituted as described on page 42.

Citrus fruit liqueurs are used extensively to enhance the flavor of appetizers, soups, meats, fish, breads, vegetables, desserts, and drinks. Because of their versatility, we suggest recipes yielding 4 cups (32 oz.), but any may be reduced by half or a third for testing.

ORANGE

Orange peels are the basis for most commercially produced orange liqueurs; the most popular are Curaçao, Cointreau, and Grand Marnier. We do not suggest the exact flavors of the well-known brands can be duplicated at home, but reasonable facsimiles can be created using orange peels, cut-up oranges, orange juice, extracts, and concentrates. New to the market is a Belgium made liqueur with a Russian heritage: Vaklova. A well-known writer described the flavor as "a special grainy scent of vodka hovering over taste tones of orange, anise and other fruits and herbs in unique and secret combination."

Curaçao has almost become a generic term for orange liqueur. The name was derived from the fruit on the island of Curaçao where the liqueur was initially produced. Today, curaçaos are made in other countries where oranges are grown, including the Antilles, Haiti, the Mediterranean countries, and South and Southwest United States. The color of the liqueur varies from orange to brown, white, green, and blue.

Cointreau, made in the heart of French fruit country, is a blend of peels from five different types of oranges imported from around the world. Grand Marnier has cognac as its base rather than vodka or brandy.

Triple Sec is a blend of oranges with cloves and cinnamon. Sabra, made in Israel, is a combination of orange and chocolate.

We have had about fifteen recipes for orange liqueurs given to us, each differing slightly by the number of oranges, by the way the peels should be cut, by the flavoring added, and by the alcohol base which can be vodka, brandy, or gin. The minor variations attest to the casual interpretation of ingredients and amounts that can be used. If you like brandy better than vodka, use it. Some recipes substitute orange juice for the peels and gin or vodka as the alcohol base. We have tried them all and our tasters decided it's a matter of personal preference.

If you like to experiment, try half recipes and steep some oranges in vodka, some in gin, some in brandy. You'll have instant variety and a basis for determining which you like best at a very nominal cost. At this writing, a bottle of brand-name orange liqueur (marked ⅘) was about $12 for 23 oz. or 52¢ per ounce. Vodka is about 8¢ per ounce; add the cost of two oranges. The savings is obvious.

To make orange liqueur, the general procedures are:

1. Prepare the flavoring and add to the alcohol base.
2. Steep 2–3 weeks; turn and shake the jar gently every few days during this time.
3. Strain and filter.
4. Add sugar syrup (or honey) and smoother (optional).
5. Let the liqueur mature.

The flavor will vary depending upon the type of oranges used. Fresh oranges with slightly green skins picked from a tree or those purchased from a health food store are ideal because they have not been chemically treated to make the skins orange.

The ripeness of the oranges and the season they are picked also result in variations of the final taste. Valencia oranges, for example, may be sweeter than Washington navel oranges. There are several varieties of mandarin oranges: Dancy, Honey, Clementine, Kara; and all may be used. Always wash fruits thoroughly. Peels should be scraped so none of the white rind remains. Blot the peels on paper towels to dry off oils and water.

Whole oranges

> 3 whole sweet oranges, cut into wedges
> ½ lemon
> 2 whole cloves
> 3 cups vodka
> 1 cup sugar syrup

Place the oranges, lemon, cloves, and vodka in a jar (vodka should cover the fruit) and steep 10 days. Strain and filter. Add sugar syrup. Mature 3–4 weeks.
Yield: 4 cups

Orange peels

> Peels only from 4 medium size oranges, scraped
> and cut into large chunks
> 3 cups vodka
> 1 cup sugar syrup

Always scrape the white rind from the peels as it can impart a bitter flavor to the liqueur. Steep 2–3 weeks. (Extra peels can be added to the mixture when you eat oranges, but they must be scraped). Strain and filter. Add sugar syrup. Let mature.
Yield: 4 cups

Orange juice

> 12 ounces (4½ cups) freshly squeezed orange juice
> Scraped and sliced peel of one orange
> 12 ounces (1½ cups) vodka or half vodka and half
>   brandy
> 1 cup sugar syrup

Combine juice, orange peel, alcohol. Steep 4 weeks. Strain and filter. Add sugar syrup.
Yield: 4 cups

Orange extract

> 1½ teaspoons extract (Be sure to use a "pure"
>   extract, not an "imitation")
> 1 pinch cinnamon
> 1 pinch caraway
> 1 pinch coriander
> 3 cups brandy or vodka
> 1 cup sugar syrup

Mix all the ingredients (including sugar syrup) in the bottle and steep a few days.
Yield: 4 cups

Optional flavorings for any or all of the above: a pinch or ¼ teaspoon cinnamon, coriander, whole cloves, or a piece of lemon rind scraped and cut.

LEMON-LIME

Liqueurs based on combinations of lemons and limes are particularly tasty in salad dressings as well as for sipping. Use them to add zest and interest to other liqueurs, too. We suggest making a full recipe: sweeten one half of the steeped fruit with enough sugar syrup to make it tasty. Use no sweetener or under-sweeten the other half for use as an eau de vie.

> Scraped and sliced peels of 4 lemons and 4 limes
> 3 cups vodka
> 1 cup sugar syrup

Steep the peels in vodka for 2 weeks. Filter. Divide into two separate bottles and add sweetener to one bottle only, if desired.
NOTE: substitute 2 teaspoons each lemon and lime extract. No steeping or filtering will be necessary.
Yield: 4 cups

DAIQUIRI WITH LIME

A bonus citrus recipe uses limes with rum as the base.

> 4 limes
> 3 cups light rum
> 1½ cups superfine granulated sugar

Pare very thinly the peel from the limes and carefully scrape away the white, and cut into strips. Blot the peel on paper towel. Steep in 2 cups of the rum for 2 days or until the rum absorbs the color from the peel. Remove the peel. Add sugar and shake vigorously until dissolved. Add remaining 1 cup of rum and stir until the liquid is clear. Mature at least 1 week.
Yield: 4 cups

TANGERINE

Tangerines are available for a short season compared to oranges, lemons, and limes so use them advantageously to make delicious liqueurs. Whole fruits, quartered fruits, and the peels only are used in the following recipes. A twist of lemon or lime peel helps to bring out the flavor.

Whole fresh fruit

> 4-5 whole tangerines
> 4 whole cloves
> 3 cups vodka
> 1 cup sugar syrup

Pierce the tangerine peelings with a fork, a knitting needle, or a skewer. Insert the cloves into some of the indentations. Steep in vodka for ten days using enough vodka to cover the fruit. Strain and filter. Add sugar syrup. Mature.
Yield: 4 cups

Tangerine peels

> 5 medium tangerine peels cut and scraped
> ½ lemon peel cut and scraped
> 3 cups vodka or half vodka and half brandy
> ½ to 1 cup sugar syrup (depending on alcohol used)

Scrape all the white from inside the peels and steep in alcohol for 3 weeks. Strain and filter. Add sugar syrup. Mature 2 months.
Yield: 4 cups

Tangerine vermouth

Try this bonus recipe with the strained out tangerine residue. Add the residue of the steeped peels or fruit to 3 cups of vermouth and let it stand for 6 months. (No sweetener is required.) Strain and filter. Mature 60 days.

Yield: 3½ cups

Optional flavorings: a pinch or up to ¼ teaspoon of cloves, cinnamon, thyme, caraway seeds, or coriander seeds.

Tangerines and brandy

> 4 medium tangerines
> 3 cups brandy

Cut the tangerines in quarters and steep in brandy for 5 weeks. Strain and filter. Sweetener may not be needed with brandy. Mature quietly 6 months before serving.

Yield: 3 cups

GRAPEFRUIT

> Scraped outer peel of 2 grapefruits cut into pieces
> 3 cups brandy
> ½ cup sugar syrup

Steep peels in brandy for 10 days. Add sugar syrup gradually by tasting and establishing a ratio of flavor to sweetener. Grapefruit sizes and flavorings imparted by the peels and tartness vary markedly, so experimentation is required.

A well-known French liqueur, Forbidden Fruit, is made from grapefruit and orange peels.

MIXED FRUIT FLAVORS

> Peels: scraped and cut—4 medium oranges, 2
>   lemons, ½ lime, 1 tangerine
>   OR
> Fruit: 3 oranges, 1 lemon, ½ lime cut into quarters
>   OR
> Juice: freshly squeezed 1¼ cups grapefruit, ½ cup
>   orange, ¼ cup lemon
>   WITH
> 3 cups vodka or brandy or gin
> 1 cup sugar syrup

Steep any of the above in any alcohol for 2 weeks.
Strain and filter. Add sugar syrup and mature 2 weeks.
Yield: 4 cups

Optional flavorings: mace, cloves, cinnamon, cardamom, vanilla.

PARFAIT AMOUR

Parfait Amour is basically a liqueur made from orange and lemon with flower petals. The comparatively complex recipe can be easily simulated with pure extracts by combining:

1½ teaspoons pure lemon extract
⅛ teaspoon pure orange extract
½" length fresh vanilla bean or ⅛ teaspoon vanilla extract
6 fresh flower petals—see pages 111-112
3 cups vodka
1½ cups sugar syrup

Steep the flavorings with the vodka for 2 weeks. Remove the vanilla bean and petals. Add sugar syrup. This is traditionally a very sweet liqueur but you can adjust the flavor to taste. Mature approximately 1 week.
Yield: 3 to 4 cups

4

Fruit Flavors

Using fresh fruits to make liqueurs is a challenging creative endeavor. Sometimes, it seems akin to discovering the who-done-it in a mystery. Liqueur-making companies have surrounded their blends with such secrecy and folderol that even the thought of trying to duplicate them is almost heresy. Nothing could be further from the truth, or the proof.

The proof we offer is that the following recipes can be loosely interpreted and readily altered to please your own discriminating taste buds. We laugh as we recall the pineapple and banana cordials we toted home from a Cuba honeymoon, hesitating to drink them for then they would be gone forever. Now we know they are as easy to create as making a milkshake, and much less costly. We think ours taste better than the store-bought blends because we have made them less sweet, less syrupy. The same is true of many other fruit liqueurs;

peach, plum, pear, cherry, the whole range of berries when they are in season.

It's easy to peel away the confusion about fruit liqueurs and categorize the flavors. The following will help you define some of the differences in the labels you find on commercial bottles:

When the words "crème de (or d')" precede the name of the fruit, it means the liqueur is sweeter than the plain variety. Example: a black currant liqueur is called "cassis"; the sweeter blend is "crème de cassis."

"Eau de vie" is the unsweetened flavored alcohol made by commercially distilling rather than steeping. For home mixing purposes, it can be made by steeping.

"Ratafia" is used synonymously with liqueurs and cordials. A cherry ratafia is a cherry liqueur.

Most of the recipes that follow are made with fresh fruits. These cannot be "exact" as the ripeness of the fruit, the variety, and the natural sugars and flavors vary. Generally, the amounts and the ingredients added should yield delicious results.

Frozen and canned fruits can be substituted for fresh fruits but because of the different amounts of sugar and juices in different brands, it is impossible to develop an all encompassing recipe. You are urged to experiment.

Dried fruits, also excellent for liqueur making, should be plumped up by placing them in boiling water to cover and allowing the fruit to sit in the hot water, with the heat turned off, for about 10 minutes until much of the water is absorbed. Pour off excess water. Cool completely and add to the alcohol.

Many fruit flavor liqueurs can be made quickly with the pure extracts and concentrates available. After mixing, these are ready for drinking in a few days; fresh fruits require longer steeping and aging periods.

Select fresh, ripe, firm fruit. In some recipes, the stones and pits are used. Whole sugar may be added to the fresh fruit and alcohol in the *initial* steeping; the sugar will chemically unite with the fruit to absorb it if the mix is placed in the sun or in a warm place and turned frequently. OR, the fruit can be steeped in the alcohol for a given period of time, then strained and filtered and the sugar syrup added. Either process will be successful with most fruits and one can be relatively loose about the recommendations given. We have tried many fruits both ways, often making half the recipe one way, half the other. Generally, we included the method we preferred and which we felt was easiest and tastiest. If you mix up the procedure on one or another, don't worry about it. Chances are the results will be delicious.

When steeping fruits, the alcohol should cover the fruit completely to preserve the fruit. If the amount of liquid given in the recipe is insufficient to cover the fruit, add a little more. It is not necessary to fill the jars as long as the fruit is covered.

When recipes call for crushed fruit pits or nuts, place the pieces in a plastic or paper bag and hit with a hammer. Crushing pits and nuts releases flavorful oils essential to the liqueur.

Many fruit liqueurs are naturally heavy and smooth so that the glycerine additive is not necessary. Decide according to your own taste.

Dare to experiment with exotic fruits you may have available in your part of the country, or those growing on your bushes and trees. If you don't have a harvest big enough for a full recipe, interpolate the amount of ingredients required for the quantity of fruit you do have. One of our friends made a 2-cup recipe from a home grown juniper berry; it was delicious. The following year, she added more shrubs to the garden so she would be assured a greater yield.

For sweetening fruit and alcohol mixes, use the sugar syrup recipe given in Chapter 2 (2 parts sugar to 1 part water). Always allow the syrup to cool before adding to alcohol; heat evaporates alcohol. When you substitute honey for sugar, use ¾ to 1 cup of honey in place of 1 cup of syrup. Honey is a little difficult to work with but mild flavors, such as orange and clove can produce different tastes. For the crème, double the amount of sweetener. To help break down the thickness of honey and make fruits easier to filter, add ⅛ teaspoon Pectic Enzyme to the solution.

We like to store sweetened liqueurs in dark beer bottles to mature; not very esthetic, but practical. If you're not a beer drinker, you can find the bottles after a Sunday picnic in a park. Wash and sterilize them before using and buy corks that fit. When a full recipe overflows the 1¾-cup beer bottle, divide the recipe in half; keep one bottle in the bar for testing and sipping, the other in the kitchen for cooking.

Whenever practical, save the strained fruits for the "Fruitueur's Fantasy" (page 23) and add sugar and alcohol as necessary.

Generally, use 80-proof vodka or an inexpensive brandy. If a 100-proof vodka is used, the sugar syrup should be increased by about ⅛. Vodka and brandy may be mixed half and half or ⅔ vodka and ⅓ brandy.

Fruit liqueurs have most often been associated with desserts. They can also impart an inspired flavoring to salad dressings, baked breads, vegetables, chicken dressings and sauces, ham, and beef. The sweetness of a fruit liqueur can be reduced by adding lemon juice or a dash of the citrus eau de vie suggested in Chapter 3. Keep a bottle on the kitchen shelf with other flavorings and you'll be amazed at how quickly the liqueur additive becomes addictive.

APPLE

Apples of one or more variety are available all year around, so you can experiment with recipes that range from the sweet, delicate flavors of Red Delicious apples to the pungent, sharp flavors of Pippins. Use the strained out liqueur-flavored apples for desserts, combine them with freshly cut apples for pies and in sweet potato and squash recipes. Each recipe will yield about 3 cups of liqueur.

Tart apples

> 1 pound slightly tart eating apples (about 3 average
>   size)
> 2 cups sugar
> 2 cloves
> Pinch of nutmeg
> Sliced and scraped peel of one lime or lemon
> 2 cups vodka or brandy

Cut ripe apples into about 8 pieces and remove the
cores but do not peel. Place all the ingredients in a
tightly closed jar and set in the sun for several days or
until all the sugar has dissolved and been absorbed.
Strain and filter. Mature for 2–3 months.

Sweet apples

> 1 pound Red Delicious or other sweet apples
> 2 cloves
> Pinch of cinnamon
> 2 cups vodka or brandy
> 1 cup sugar syrup

Cut apples in halves or quarters and remove the cores
but do not peel. Place apples, cloves, cinnamon, and
alcohol in a bottle and let steep for 2 weeks. Strain and
filter. Add sugar syrup. Mature 2–3 months.

APRICOT

Apricot liqueurs have the distinctive, strong flavor of
the fruit, a delightful bouquet, and a jewel-like amber
color. A light almond flavor and aroma are subtly
discernible, imparted from the nut inside the apricot pit
or by adding crushed almonds or almond extract. The
alcohol base can be vodka or a combination of two parts
vodka and one part brandy. For Crème d'Abricot,

double the sugar syrup recipe. Glycerine is optional. Each recipe will yield 3-4 cups (24-32 ounces). They may be halved.

Fresh apricots

 1 pound fresh apricots
 3 cups vodka
 1 cup sugar syrup

Cut apricots in half and remove pits. Place the pits in a plastic or paper bag, and hit them with a hammer to open. Remove the inner nut and discard the pit covers. Place the nuts in a bag and hit them to crush them and release the flavorful oils. (Any trace of the pit covering can impart a bitter taste.) Combine the fruit and nuts in alcohol. Steep two weeks, and shake gently two or three times a week. Strain and squeeze all the juice from the fruit. Filter until clear. Add sugar syrup. Mature 2-3 months.

Dried apricots

 ½ pound dried pitted apricots
 1 cup boiled water (approximately)
 5 whole almonds, or 1 teaspoon almond extract
  used for baking
 2-3 cups vodka or brandy
 1 cup sugar syrup

Plump apricots by soaking in just enough boiling water to cover them. (Bring water to boil, turn off, and soak fruit about 10 minutes or until water is absorbed.) Cool. Pour off any remaining liquid and measure; add enough vodka to make a total of three cups. Combine apricot liquid, apricots, almond. Steep 2 weeks, shaking occasionally. Filter. Add sugar syrup.

Canned apricots

> 1 1-pound size (16 ounces) canned apricots with
>   pits prepared as in recipe for fresh apricots
>   (above)
> 5 crushed almonds or 1 teaspoon almond extract
> 1-3 cups vodka
> ½ cup sugar syrup

Prepare the canned apricots, pits, and nuts as for fresh apricots. Strain the juice, measure, and add to the vodka to equal three cups. Combine fruit, almonds, vodka for one to two weeks steeping. Strain and filter. If presweetened canned apricots are used, taste the strained liquid before adding sugar syrup as you may not want more sweetening, or perhaps only a little bit.

Optional flavorings: A pinch of cinnamon or cinnamon stick, a pinch of cloves or two whole cloves, a two- to three-inch square of fresh coconut, ¼ cup flaked coconut, or a drop of coconut extract; small piece of sliced and scraped lemon peel. Add the strained fruit to your "Fruitueur's Fantasy."

BANANA

Given the availability of bananas, you can keep a ready supply of this heady tasting liqueur all the time. Banana liqueur is so easy to make and costs about 70% less than the commercial variety. Mix it dry or sweet, serve it in small glasses as a delightful aperitif, or pour it over ice cream, mix it with non-dairy whip, add it to the liquid when baking muffins, breads, and cakes. Mix up extra batches for sure-to-please housewarming gifts. For Crème de Banana, double the amount of sugar syrup in the recipe below.

> 2 medium-size bananas, peeled
> 1 teaspoon vanilla extract or a 2″ length of vanilla bean
> 1 cup sugar syrup
> 3 cups vodka

Mash the bananas and add the vanilla and cooled sugar syrup to the vodka. Shake gently. Steep 1 week. Strain and filter. It may be consumed now, but a two to three month maturing period will result in a richer flavor. Yield: 4 cups

Optional flavorings: a pinch of cloves, a piece of cinnamon stick.

BERRY

Use berries as freshly picked as possible. If frozen berries are substituted, compensate for the frozen juice by using less sugar syrup. The recipes given yield between 3-4 cups of finished liqueur. When the quantities of fresh berries are not sufficient for a full recipe, reduce the alcohol and sugar syrup amounts accordingly. You can mix fresh and frozen berries.

Blackberry, blueberry, elderberry, huckleberry, juniper berry

All may be used the same way.

> 4 cups fresh berries
> Sliced and scraped peel of one lemon
> Pinch of tarragon or cloves
> 3 cups vodka or 2 cups vodka and 1 cup brandy or sweet white wine
> 1 cup sugar syrup

Lightly crush berries with a fork. Add to vodka with lemon peel and cloves. Steep 3 months. Strain. Crush the berries through the filters to squeeze out all the juices. Add sugar syrup to taste. Mature 4–6 weeks.

Frozen berry liqueurs

When fresh berries are unavailable, you can make liqueurs with frozen berries. We suggest experimenting with one 10-ounce package of any berries and making small batches.

> 1 10-ounce package strawberries, raspberries, or any berry
> 1½ cups vodka or 1 cup vodka and ½ cup brandy
> ¼ cup sugar syrup

Add juice and berries to alcohol. Stir and steep one week. Strain. Crush berries through strainer and filter. Taste. Add sugar syrup as necessary. Many frozen fruits are already heavily pre-sugared. If using unsugared fruits without syrup treat them as fresh fruits, but reduce the amount of water when making the sugar syrup because of the water content in the frozen fruits. Yield: about 2 cups

Cranberry

   1 pound fresh cranberries
   Sliced and scraped peel of ¼ orange
   Sliced and scraped peel of ½ lemon
   1½ cups sugar syrup
   1½ cups vodka

Wash cranberries and coarsely chop in blender or food processor. Add all the ingredients to the alcohol. Steep 4 weeks. Strain and filter. If more sweetener is required, add more sugar syrup to taste and mature another week.

Raspberry brandy

   1½ cups ripe raspberries
   Sliced and scraped peel of ½ lemon
   3 cups vodka or 3 cups brandy or 2 parts vodka and
       1 part brandy, or substitute white wine for the
       brandy
   ¾ cup sugar syrup

Lightly crush berries, add lemon peel and berries to alcohol. Steep 2-4 weeks. Strain and filter, squeezing all the berries through the fine cloth. Add the sugar syrup and mature 4-6 weeks.

   For Crème de Framboise, use all brandy and add 2 cups of sugar syrup.

Raspberry and gin

   2 pounds fresh raspberries lightly crushed
   2 pounds sugar
   3 cups gin

Mix all the ingredients together. Turn every day until the sugar is dissolved. Strain. Drink and enjoy.

Strawberry

> 3 cups fresh strawberries cut into thirds. Wild and cultivated strawberries will yield different flavors: wild strawberries result in a stronger and more distinct strawberry flavor, but they are not readily available.
> 3 tablespoons powdered sugar
> 3 cups vodka
> 1 cup sugar syrup

Remove stems from berries. Sprinkle powdered sugar on berries and let dissolve; then add to alcohol. Steep 2 weeks. Crush the berries through the strainer. Filter. Add syrup and mature one week. Filter again through coarse to fine cloth and the liqueur is ready to drink.

For Crème de Fraises, add 2 cups sugar syrup.
Yield: 5 cups

Red fruit ratafia

Gather a medley of red fruits: cherries, red currants, raspberries, and mulberries. Slightly mash them and leave them in a covered jar in a cool place for 3 days. Strain and measure the juice; add an equal amount of brandy to the juice. For each pint of juice/brandy liquid, add ¼ cup sugar syrup and one length of cinnamon stick. Add the fruit and steep for 2 months. Strain and filter. Add more sugar syrup if necessary. Mature 4-6 weeks. Add all strained crushed berries to the "Fruitueur's Fantasy" or make a separate "Berry Fantasy" and add sugar and alcohol as needed. This residue is elegant over puddings, in parfaits, yogurt dishes, pies, muffins, and as toppings for ice cream.

CHERRY

Cherries, with their luscious color, delicious flavors, and many varieties vie for top popularity among all liqueurs. Cherry and orange flavors statistically account for more than half of all fruit liqueurs sold today. Next in popularity are apricot, blackberry, and raspberry.

Cherry Heering is probably the first that comes to mind. It's a lip smacking flavor made in Denmark from a small Danish black cherry and named for the man who first created it in 1818, Peter F. Heering. Crème de Cerise is a cherry liqueur made in France; Cherry Suisse is a combination of cherries and Swiss chocolate.

Kirsch, or kirschwasser, is a cherry eau de vie; an unsweetened distillate of fermented cherries. There is Cherry Marnier, a light French liqueur; Maraschino, made from Italian maraschino cherries, is sweet and highly concentrated. Cerasalla, another Italian liqueur, owes its distinctive rich flavor to a combination of cherries and herbs gathered in the Abruzzi mountains. Wishniak is a cherry liqueur from Israel. Japan makes a cherry blossom liqueur.

People have shared many cherry flavored liqueur recipes with us. We have only found Bing cherries in our grocery stores so had to confine our liqueur making to those. Canned and frozen cherries have not proven particularly tasty and not worth the effort as a drink. In England, liqueur-making enthusiasts raise specific types of cherry trees to yield the tart cherries they use in their own liqueurs.

To prepare cherries, wash thoroughly and remove the stems. Blot on paper toweling to dry. When a recipe calls for whole cherries, pierce the skins with a darning needle, skewer, or fork down to the stone. The alcohol should permeate to the stone which imparts additional desirable flavor. You can vary the alcohol base by using all vodka, all brandy, or ⅔ brandy and ⅓ vodka. Combine the steeping cherries with other flavors (1 teaspoon mint, chocolate extract, coconut, or all three) to simulate commercial liqueur flavors such as Sabra and CocoRibe. You can also combine two or three flavors of finished liqueurs to concoct a new combination. When combining finished liqueurs, shake them well, and let mature a few weeks, shaking frequently to intermix. Try varying quantities of each in small batches to determine the combinations you like best.

All cherry liqueurs are excellent served straight, on the rocks, in frappés, as portions of the liquid in baking recipes, on ham, pork, and duck, in sauces and over desserts. Inject them into candies with hypodermic needles (see Part 2, page 181).

Cherry Wishniak

½ pound large unblemished Bing cherries
½ pound granulated sugar
2 cups vodka or brandy

Wash and stem the cherries and place them on a towel to dry. Gently put the cherries into a 1-quart jar. Pour the sugar over the cherries. *Do not stir or shake.* Pour the vodka or brandy over the sugar and the cherries. Do not stir. Cover tightly with a lid and put the jar on a high shelf. Let it stand for 3 months without stirring or shaking. Strain into a 1-quart bottle. The cherry meat will be dissolved. No sugar syrup is added, so the alcohol content will be high. The color is beautiful and the taste is divine.
Yield: 2½–3 cups

Almost any other fresh fruit may be substituted in this recipe. Use apples, peaches, apricots, plums, peeled oranges, and tangerines. We have been told that "handed down" recipes call for covering the jar with cheesecloth, but fruit flies develop. It may be O.K. but not to our tastes.

Cherry mint liqueur

You'll need a little sunshine to help this recipe along but it's worth the effort, especially with cherries in season during the warm weather. Use it with or without the mint.

> 2½ cups sweet Bing cherries, pitted
> 10 crushed cherry stones
> 10 fresh mint leaves or 2 tablespoons dried mint (1 tablespoon mint extract can be substituted)
> Sliced peel of ½ lemon
> 2 cups vodka
> ½ cup sugar (not sugar syrup)

Remove the stems from the cherries, cut in half, and remove the pits. Crush the cherries lightly. Crush about 10 of the cherry stones by placing them in a plastic or cloth bag and hitting with a hammer. Place crushed pits and cherries in a quart jar. Add the sugar, then the vodka. Close the jar tightly and place in the sun daily for 1 week. Then set the jar in a cool dark place for 4 weeks. Strain. Let mature at least 2 months.
Yield: 3-4 cups

Optional flavorings: add 5 cloves, ½″ stick of cinnamon, or a pinch of mace.

Whole cherry liqueur

Always be sure the fruit is thoroughly covered with the liquid.

    2 pounds or about 2½ cups ripe Bing cherries
    2 tablespoons powdered sugar
    Sliced and scraped peel of ½ lemon
    2 cups brandy
    1 cup vodka
    ½ cup sugar syrup

Pull stems from half of the cherries. Cut the stems from the other half of the cherries just at the top so the inner fruit is exposed. Pierce all the cherries down to the stones with four or five holes. Place cherries in quart (liter) jar. Sprinkle with powdered sugar and let dissolve. Add lemon peel. Shake gently. Add brandy and vodka to cover. Close jar and store in a warm place about 75° for 6 weeks undisturbed. Strain and filter. Squeeze all the juice from the cherries. Add sugar syrup. Shake well. Mature for at least 1 week.
Yield: approximately 4 cups

Optional flavors: 5 cloves, ½ piece cinnamon stick, or 1 pinch mace.

    Save the strained cherries and add to "Fruitueur's Fantasy" or the "Berry Fantasy."

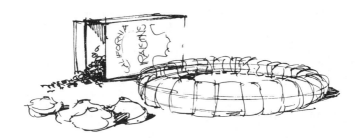

CURRANT AND RAISIN

Black currants, tiny delicious fruits with a raisin-like flavor are the basis for the sweet, clear amber-colored cassis and crème de cassis usually served as an after-dinner liqueur. Crème de cassis is commercially made by steeping the fruit in brandy, but it is also delicious with a vodka base. Use it often for the popular French cocktail Kir (page 134) or add the liqueur to fruitcakes, puddings, or for basting over ham when a raisin sauce is called for.

We have successfully used California black and golden raisins in the same recipe for our own variety of liqueur . . . each with a slightly different degree of sweetness and flavoring.

Always save the strained out currants and raisins for the "Fruitueur's Fantasy." You may wish to retain the currants and raisins separately to make jellies and jams, or to spread on the bottom of pie shells before adding other fruits and puddings.

We suggest a small recipe first since it's so easy to recreate. Establish the sweetness and amount of flavoring from the currants or raisins you have available, then make your next batch in larger quantities.

> 1 cup water
> 1 cup currants (or raisins)
> 2 cups vodka or brandy
> ¾ cup sugar syrup for cassis. Use 1¼ cups sugar
>   syrup for creme de cassis

Boil 1 cup water. Add currants. Cover and turn off heat and let currants plump up in the hot water for about 5 minutes. Strain off water. Place currants and alcohol in a tightly closed jar and steep for 1 week. Shake the jar occasionally during the week. Strain and filter. Add ¼ cup sugar syrup for cassis, 1¼ cups for crème de cassis, or to taste. Mature for two weeks. You can divide this

recipe and make half cassis and half crème de cassis.
Yield: 3-4½ cups
NOTE: We have sometimes added the cooled sugar syrup
to steep with the fruit and vodka and it hasn't seemed to
make any difference in the final product.

DATE AND FIG

Certain fresh fruits are more easily available in different parts of the country. Fresh dates and figs are abun-
dant in Southern California so we have ample oppor-
tunity to try them in different recipes. Having access to
a wide variety also makes it possible to vary the tastes
and we have never missed, though some dates are
sweeter and heavier than others. We have tried packaged dried dates and figs, available seasonally in other
parts of the country, and have asked our test recipe
makers to do the same. All report excellent drinks using
approximately the following proportions.

The fruits are inherently very sweet so reduce the
amount of sugar syrup and only add to the mix in
graduated proportions as you taste it.

> 2½ cups (1 pound) cut up dates (pitted) or figs, or
> combine 1 cup of each for a date-fig liqueur.
> 2 cups vodka
> ¼-½ cup sugar syrup

Plump up dried fruits by placing them in boiled water
for 5 minutes. Drain the excess water. Cut fruit into
smaller pieces with a scissors or sharp knife. Place the
cooled fruit in the vodka for 2 weeks, shake occasionally. Strain and filter. Add sugar syrup to taste.
Yield: 2½ cups

PAPAYA, MANGO, AND MELON

Each season, as different fruits come into your stores from various parts of the world, keep your recipe imagination honed. For example, the texture of papaya, mango, and cantaloupe are much like peaches, pears, and plums and may be used similarly for liqueurs. The results, however, are different and delicious tasting!

Papaya is a large, oblong yellow edible fruit grown in tropical climates. It is used much as a cantaloupe or other melon but is more often associated with jellies and preserves than liqueurs. It is surprising that it is not a liqueur, as it is the source of the drug Papain, an enzyme similar to pepsin which helps to digest food. Its inherent flavor is mildly sweet with a difficult to describe, characteristically pleasant tang. Those who are familiar with the fruit have been able to identify the liqueur by its tangy bouquet. Try mangos and cantaloupes, crenshaw and honeydew melons, too.

The following test-size recipe will yield about 1½ cups liqueur. The same recipe may be used for all the melons, then adjustments made to taste.

> ½ medium-size ripe melon cut into pieces to make about 1 cup
> Scraped and cut up peel of ¼ lemon or lime
> 1 cup vodka
> ⅓ cup sugar syrup

Cut the melon in half, remove the peeling and seeds as you would a cantaloupe. Cut in ½″ pieces. Place the cut-up fruit pieces in the vodka and steep 1 week. Strain and squeeze the softened fruit to extract as much juice as possible. Add the sugar syrup. Mature 3 weeks.

The squeezed out fruit remains are usually too soft to add to the "Fruitueur's Fantasy." Keep it in a separate small jar, add sugar, and spoon over ice cream or eat plain. Use the resulting liqueur in any cooking recipe that calls for a fruit flavor.

PEACH

Peaches, easy to find and inexpensive in season, are perfect for liqueurs that will delight guests all year around. Add the liqueur to mixed drinks, to punches, and a variety of recipes. Serve it in small cordial glasses on a cocktail table in front of a glowing fire and watch the flickering flames' reflection in the amber tones.

So sure are we of the palate pleasing success that we suggest a large recipe while the fruits are in season. Then let the liqueur mature so you have it to drink all year long. It improves with age. Add more sugar syrup to a portion of the recipe to result in crème de pêche.

> 10 medium-size ripe peaches
> 3 cups vodka
> 1 cup sugar syrup

Pare the skin, cut the fruit into quarters, discard the skin and the peach stones. Place the cut up peaches in vodka in a tightly covered jar for 1 week and shake a few times. Filter and strain. Squeeze all juices from the fruit. Add the sugar syrup. Mature 4 to 6 weeks.
Yield: 4 cups

Optional flavorings: 2-3 cloves, lemon peel.

In gourmet liquor and food shops, you will sometimes see a bottle of peach liqueur with a large peach inside surrounded by the liqueur. You know it is impossible to force such a large fruit through the neck of the bottle. How is it done? The farmer places the bottle over the fruit growing on the tree. Then the peach grows and ripens within the bottle. The farmer carefully removes the bottle with the peach branch and leaves. The liqueur is made, then poured over the fruit and the bottle is sealed with the large peach immersed within.

Southern Comfort, an American liqueur, is based on peaches, bourbon, and several secret ingredients. Any peach flavored liqueur is a marvelous addition to punch drinks, chicken recipes, and a multitude of desserts.

PEAR

Different pear varieties are in season at various times of the year so watch for them on your grocery counters: the green-yellow Bartlett, the brown Russet d'Anjou, or the popular Kieffer, for example. Any and all may be used for making fresh pear liqueurs. Consider your recipes your personal label, Poire or Crème de Poire. Add sweeteners to taste for delectable, smooth-on-the-tongue products that will win rave notices from your most critical testers.

Pears are in the same family as apples. Any flavorings or combinations you associate with apple pies, cobblers, and sauces may be used with pears, such as cinnamon, nutmeg, cloves, or allspice.

Pear liqueur is so easy to make, we offer a small test recipe for 1½ cups to 2 cups.

When the taste promises to please make additional recipes. Mix when ripe firm pears first appear on the market. Steep about 10 days. Sweeten and taste. Adjust the recipe as necessary, then you're ready to stock up on pears and make enough bottles of pear liqueur to enjoy all year long.

½ pound mature ripe firm pears
2 apples—peels only (any variety, we like Red
       Delicious)
1 clove
½″ cinnamon stick or pinch of cinnamon
Pinch nutmeg
2 coriander seeds
1 cup granulated sugar
1½ cups vodka or brandy

Cut the pears in strips (do not pare) and place in a jar
with all the other dry ingredients including sugar and
the apple peels. Add alcohol to cover. Steep 2 weeks.
Shake the jar every two days to mix the ingredients.
Strain and filter. If you like the liqueur sweeter, add
sugar syrup in small quantities (about 1 ounce to 4
ounces liqueur) to establish a sweetness ratio. Then add
to the whole bottle accordingly. When the recipe tastes
perfect (and you have recorded it in your recipe file)
purchase more pears and make larger amounts for
cooking, drinking, and gift giving. Mature about 2
months.

PINEAPPLE

If pineapple liqueur suggests hip-swinging dancers from
Hawaii, then make up a recipe as quickly as the drums
beat. Fresh pineapples are tastiest when they are in
season. They are delightfully sweet and juicy by nature
and so easy to make into liqueurs, using any or all of the
following recipes. Each will yield 3 to 3½ cups.

Pineapple with rum

½ pound fresh pineapple (about 1¼ cups)
3 cups rum

Use a fresh, ripe pineapple. Peel. Cut up the pineapple meat into small pieces and place in a jar with the rum. Steep for 3 weeks. Strain and filter. Mature at least 1 month.

Pineapple slices with brandy

Select 1 medium-size ripe pineapple. Peel. Cut the pineapple into thin slices. Use a wide-mouth canning jar and place the pineapple slices in the jar one on top of the other in the same shape as the pineapple. Add sugar until it reaches half the height of the fruit. Cover with brandy to reach the top of the fruit, though the jar need not be full. There should be more brandy than sugar. Steep for 2 months. Strain and filter. Mature 1 month.

Pineapple with vodka

2 cups fresh, cut up pineapple
¼ teaspoon pure vanilla flavoring or about 1″ fresh
    vanilla bean cut and split
2½ cups vodka
½ cup sugar syrup

Combine the pineapple, vanilla, and vodka in a jar and let steep about 1 week. Strain and squeeze out all the juice from the pineapple by mashing it through the strainer. Filter, then sweeten with sugar syrup and filter through finer mesh filters, if any pulp remains. To make the liqueur sweeter, if necessary, add sweetened pineapple juice or small quantities of sugar syrup. Mature 1 month.

PLUM AND PRUNE

Select firm ripe plums to make sweet, smooth amber liqueurs that slide on your tongue and warm your throat. Use the sweet, small purple plums or the large, meaty tart plums fresh from the grocer's counter or plucked from the tree. When plums are out of season, substitute prunes which are dried plums. Incidentally, prunelle and crème de prunelle (a plum-prune taste) are made from a small berry-like variety of wild plum, known as the "sloeberry" in the United States and as the "Blackthorn" in England.

Plum

> 1 pound fresh plums, cut up or used whole
> 3 cloves
> ¼" piece of cinnamon stick or pinch of cinnamon
> 1 cup sugar
> 2 cups vodka

Place cut up plums and pits or whole plums (pierce the skins to the pit) in a jar with flavorings, sugar, and vodka. Be sure vodka covers the plums. Steep 3 months, shaking occasionally to mix all the ingredients. Strain. Enjoy the fruit as a dessert as it has been sweetened and has the whole liqueur flavor.

> OR

Place the plums and flavorings in the vodka without the sugar. Steep 10 days.

Strain and filter the plums, then add ¾ cup sugar syrup; ½ pound dried prunes may be substituted in either of these recipes instead of the plums.

Prunes in brandy

> ½ pound large prunes with or without pits
> Scraped and sliced peel from ¼ orange
> 1" piece of cinnamon stick
> ¾ cup sugar syrup
> 2 cups brandy (or enough to cover the prunes)

Add all the ingredients in a jar. (It is not necessary to plump the prunes.) Steep 4 weeks. Strain out the prunes and use as a dessert. Filter the liqueur. Mature 2–3 months. Try this with other flavored brandies such as grape or a mixture of ⅔ brandy and ⅓ red wine.

The strained fruits are excellent additions for the "Fruitueur's Fantasy" but be sure to remove any pits.

5

Herbs and Spices

Scores of books have been written about herbs and spices. Their use in foods and for medicines is so ancient that their history is impossible to trace with real accuracy. Records that remain indicate, for example, that the ancient Greeks and Romans toasted their gods with a drink, made of wine, honey, and spices, called "hippocras." In those early centuries plants, herbs, and spices used for medicinal purposes were made more palatable by combining them with alcoholic beverages.

Early Oriental and Indian civilizations used herbs and spices extensively as did some European cultures. Their use in France and Italy expanded greatly during the Middle Ages when trade routes from the Far East opened up and the rare plants were brought to Europe. Experiments with the medicinal plants by French alchemists during the high Renaissance became the basis for many of the liqueurs we know today. The monks of the Carthusian, Benedictine, and Cistercian orders with scientific leanings appear to have dedicated their lives to the development of liqueur recipes that remain as guarded in this century as the day they were developed.

Many herb liqueurs produced today are based on multiple flavorings with anywhere from a dozen to a hundred ingredients. Best known are: "Benedictine" of France which has a dominant angelica flavor; "Galliano" of Italy; "Grand Gruyère" of Switzerland; and the Spanish "Cuarenta y Tres" (43) which, logically, is composed of a blend of 43 herbs and plants.

Through the years, competitive liqueur producers have tried to imitate these well-known brands. Some have come close though, by law, none can use the same name. That is why you will find labels such as "Dictine" or "Gaetano" and similar takeoffs from the trademarked brands.

Herb and spice liqueurs are easy to make with an almost 100% success guarantee. They are more accurate to reproduce than fruit liqueurs because the flavors remain the same and reliable. Fruits vary in the amount of sweetness and flavor while a teaspoon of anise, or angelica, or other, will always result in the same amount of flavoring to a given ratio of alcohol and sweetener.

The flavor potential of herbs and spices is quite strong so minimal amounts are needed; as little as ¼ teaspoon to 2 tablespoons, sometimes only a pinch of this and that. Taste preferences for these liqueurs are so varied that we suggest making them in 2- to 2½-cup quantities until you determine your favorites. Then make more. Smaller quantities are easy to store and require less vodka which is the major cost factor in any of the recipes. For larger quantities, double or triple the recipe.

Processed and dried herbs and spices should be as fresh as possible; long storage periods tend to dissipate the flavors. We prefer to buy them at a busy health-food store where the turnover is great; a few ounces may cost only 25¢–50¢ and provide more than we could use in several mixes. If you lack such a source, buy boxed spices from a busy grocery store. Always store spices in airtight, small covered jars or cans. Watch them carefully as they sometimes generate tiny bugs.

Many herbs should be crushed or broken before they are added to alcohol; a process which releases the flavors. They can be ground, broken, smashed with a pestle in a mortar, or with the back of a spoon against a cup. Or wrap the herb in heavy waxed paper and smash with a hammer or rock. Some may be ground in a blender or chopped in a food processor.

Freshly grown herbs are marvelous to use, especially if they come from your own garden. Substitute 1 table-spoon fresh chopped herbs for ⅓ teaspoon powdered or ½ teaspoon crushed dried herbs.

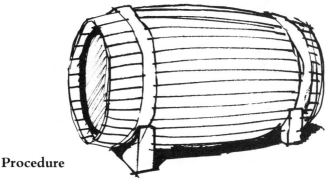

Procedure

The procedure is as easy as steeping tea. Place the prepared herbs in the alcohol base for the specific length of time, usually a week or so. Shake the bottle and turn it over occasionally to keep the flavorings suspended in the alcohol. Strain out the herbs. Then add the sweet-ener. We have not found a practical use for the herbs as we have with fruits. The addition of glycerine is op-tional.

Herbs and spices available in cans and jars on your grocer's shelves, in boxes and fresh where health foods and produce are sold. Leaves, stems, roots, seeds, pods are used from different plants. Shown are cinnamon sticks, caraway, cardamom, cinnamon, cloves, anise, ginger root, star anise, fennel.

Among the plus factors of making herb liqueurs is that you can add more flavoring if a mix is too weak and let it resteep. If it is too strong, you can dilute the solution with more alcohol. Flavored extracts can be used in conjunction with the herbs.

Generally leaves and flower petals release their flavors quickly, resulting in a shorter steeping time than needed for barks, seeds, and roots.

For the 2½-cup recipes given use ½ cup sugar syrup made by boiling together and dissolving:

½ cup sugar ⎫
¼ cup water ⎭   ½ cup sugar syrup

Honey may be used by substituting ½ to ⅝ cup mild-flavored honey for ½ cup sugar syrup. Honey will produce a cloudy liqueur that you may wish to siphon (see Chapter 2).

Different parts of different herbs are used for different purposes such as:

Allspice is valued for its berries
Balm and sage are valued for their leaves
Fennel for its seeds
Mint for its leaves
Vanilla for its pods

If you are accustomed to a limited number of herbs and spices on your condiment shelf, learning about the different varieties and how they may be used in recipes is a giant bonus of liqueur making. We recall the first time we looked for melissa, hyssop, star anise, and anise root. We thought we were treading on exotic ground. Since then, a dash of anise liqueur is added to almost all our meat-based soups. A few teaspoons of allspice liqueur is added to gelatin when it is used to mold vegetables. Once we thought caraway seed was something sported only on the tops of rye bread; today we use it extensively in the liqueur "kümmel" which we add to many cooked vegetables.

You may wish to grow your own herbs and use them fresh from your garden. However you proceed, always be willing to experiment, blend, add, and subtract flavors like a chemist searching for a new elixir. After all, that's what the commercial chemists do. They are constantly seeking new combinations, new taste experiences. They have to worry about the commercial value, where to obtain large quantities of the flavors, production costs, and shelf life. We don't. We can do our own thing and have fun, enjoyment, and the satisfaction of being creative.

ALLSPICE

Ground or whole allspice may be found on the grocer's shelf or in a health-food store. Allspice, made from the unripe berry of a tree in the myrtle family, has been around ever since Christopher Columbus discovered it in the New World and brought it back to Europe. It was named "allspice" because its aroma suggests a blend of cinnamon, cloves, and nutmeg. If allspice berries are available, crush them to achieve a coarse mix.

Allspice liqueur

¾ teaspoon allspice
1½ cups vodka or brandy
½ cup sugar syrup

Steep allspice in alcohol for 10 days. Strain and filter.
Add sugar syrup. Mature 3-4 weeks.
Yield: 2 cups

All spices and herbs

The allspice berry (above) contains the flavors mentioned. You can create a delicious takeoff by combining many spices for your private blend. We have made liqueurs with 25 different herbs when we have had bits of several left over. Generally, use a pinch of anything you have: ground spices, a few bits of the leaves from lemon, mint, bay, 2-3 coriander seeds. When you have a total content of about 2 teaspoons of flavorings add it all to:

1½ cups vodka
½ cup any dry white wine
¾ cup sugar syrup

Steep about 2 weeks. Shake occasionally. Filter and add
¾ cups sugar syrup. Mature several months.
Yield: 2 to 2¾ cups

ANGELICA

Angelica, a species of the carrot family, figures in the lore and folk tales of many countries. Its proliferation throughout Europe has made the herb an essential ingredient of medicines, perfumes, tonics, and teas as well as liqueurs. Benedictine, Galliano, Strega, and Drambuie all have angelica in the recipes.

When you attempt to simulate any of the above brand name liqueurs with your own recipes, begin with the herb angelica, available in a root form, or boxed or canned as dried and chopped pieces. The stem of the plant may also be used. Any of the optional flavorings listed below will give the drink the pungency found in many commercially made products. Use them very sparingly in the initial solution with the angelica and alcohol; you can always add more.

> ½ ounce cut up bits of angelica root or stems
> ½ ounce chopped almonds or almond extract
> 1½ cups alcohol
> ½ cup sugar syrup

Steep the cut up angelica and almond extract in alcohol 5 days. Filter and strain. Add sugar syrup or honey. Mature 2 months.
Yield: 2 cups

Optional flavorings: pinch of nutmeg, mace, cinnamon, 1 clove, 1½ teaspoons hyssop, lemon verbena; use any or all. Yellow food coloring optional. Use the finished liqueur in any food recipe that calls for Galliano or angelica.

ANISE AND LICORICE

Anise is a plant that yields seeds, leaves, and roots with a delightful licorice-like flavor. Liqueur makers have used it for centuries as the basis for anisette. Anise seed is sold as a condiment on your grocer's shelves; it is a basic for bakers and candymakers. It is also used to flavor pickles, fruit salads, soups, marinades, and teas. It has both a sweet and pungent flavor.

Other plants impart similar flavors; these include fennel seed, licorice root, star anise (a different plant than anise; the usable dried part is actually shaped like a star). The Italian liqueur Sambuca is developed from a white flowered elder bush, *Sambucus nigra,* and its flavor is so similar to anise that the anise seed is used as an accompaniment. Some anise flavored alcoholic beverages are used as substitutes for absinthe which traditionally used wormwood as an ingredient. Wormwood was banned in most countries at the turn of the century because of allegedly undesirable, unhealthy side effects.

Anise liqueur will add more zip and zest to food recipes calling for anise than the herbs alone. Make the liqueurs from anise seed, star anise (from your health food store), and licorice root and let your own taste buds decide which you like best. We suggest making small batches for comparison, then mix up your favorites in larger quantities. Each of the following recipes yields 2 cups.

Anise seed

> ⅔ tablespoon anise seed
> ½ teaspoon fennel seed
> ½ teaspoon coriander seed
> 1½ cups vodka
> ½ cup sugar syrup

Grind the seed in a mortar and steep in vodka for 1 week. Shake frequently. Add sugar syrup. Enjoy.

Licorice root

> 2½ tablespoons chopped licorice root
> 1½ cups vodka
> ½ cup sugar syrup to taste

Wash and chop the root into small pieces. Steep in vodka for 1 week. Strain and filter. Add sugar syrup.

Star anise

> ⅔ tablespoon star anise broken and crushed
> 1½ cups (12 ounces) vodka
> ½ cup sugar syrup

Steep the herb in the vodka about 2 weeks. Filter. Add sugar syrup. When completed place an "in tact" whole star in a clear glass bottle as a visual effect and conversation piece; add liqueur.

Optional spices: a pinch of mace, cinnamon.

After we made all three recipes, we mixed 2 ounces of each together in a separate bottle and the result was a heightened flavor and aroma. Very good.

CINNAMON

Spices on your cooking shelf may be imaginatively used as the basis for liqueur flavors that can be surprisingly delicious. Let them lead you to experiment with other spices like a mad alchemist. Once we discovered what could be made with coriander and caraway seeds we added other spices we found on the grocery shelf and tried those, too. Mix and match ingredients to create your own "label." We guarantee someone will like the flavors and you'll have fun creating them and using them in your cooking.

Cinnamon-coriander

> 2″ cinnamon stick or 1½ tablespoons ground
>   cinnamon
> 1½ teaspoons ground coriander seed
> 2 cloves
> 1½ cups vodka, or half and half vodka and brandy
> ½ cup sugar syrup

Steep the herbs in the alcohol for 10 days. Strain and filter. Add sugar syrup. This is especially good with brown sugar syrup. For another flavoring, add a few raisins or currants to the vodka and a slice of scraped lemon peel.

GINGER

Ginger flavored liqueurs, like ginger snaps and ginger flavored candies, are innocent enough on a first taste; but after a few seconds, they pack a powerful aftertaste. Imagine the impact of ginger tea, a homemade remedy for stomach ache in the old days.

The herb can be used innocently though when you think of its use in gingerale, ginger beer, and gingerbread. It's a versatile herb that must be used cautiously and with a delicate hand. Other flavorings may be added.

Ginger is available in 4 different forms; all may be used for steeping in vodka, brandy, or whiskey.

Ground Ginger—available in cans on grocer's condiment shelves. It is used in baking; a pinch in coffee is delicious.

Whole Dried Ginger Root—usually found in health food and gourmet cooking stores; all or pieces may be ground and cut up for cooking and baking.

Whole Dried Ginger Root—is the dominant taste in Indian and Chinese cooking; it is also used in pickles and preserves. Because fresh ginger root tends to spoil quickly, it should be frozen and bits of it cut off as needed.

Crystallized Ginger—is used in chutneys, preserves, or eaten as candy or as a topping for desserts.

Ginger liqueur

> ½ teaspoon dried ginger or 1 teaspoon fresh ginger
> 1½ cups vodka or brandy or whiskey
> ¾ cup sugar syrup

Steep the ginger in the alcohol for 1 week, shaking occasionally. Strain and filter. Add sugar syrup.
Yield: 2¼ cups

Optional flavorings: 1 cardamom seed, 1 clove, a pinch of cinnamon, a few raisins, ½ teaspoon almond extract.

KUMMEL-CARAWAY

Breathe in the aroma emanating from a bottle of kümmel liqueur and you'll probably conjure up visions of delicatessen stores and bakeries when rye bread was sold without wrappers or baked on the premises. Kümmel, to those who know liqueurs, is almost synonymous with caraway seed from which it is distilled in commercial production. But it can be made by the maceration process described below to yield a dry, clear simulation of the real thing.

The caraway seed, a little crescent-shaped herb that grows in a mound of carrot-like leaves, was used to cure the fickleness of lovers in ancient times. It is also the basis of Aquavit, an unsweetened combination of caraway and brandy made in Scandanavia by distillation. Other drinks associated with caraway and kümmel are Danzig, Danzigwasser, and Goldwasser; these may be simulated by building on the basic kummel-caraway recipe below and adding small amounts of coriander, cinnamon, lemon peel, and other spices. Goldwasser derives its name from the practice of adding gold leaf to liqueurs in medieval times when gold was believed to cure rheumatism and arthritis.

Kümmel-caraway liqueur

>   1 tablespoon caraway seed
>   1 whole clove
>   1½ cups vodka
>   ½ cup sugar syrup

Crush the caraway seeds lightly with a mortar and pestle on a board or in a cup with the back of a spoon; add the cloves and combine with vodka. Steep 2 weeks. Strain and filter. Add the sugar syrup, the caraway seed, and cloves.
      OR
To the recipe above, add to the caraway seed and cloves:

>   1½ teaspoons fennel seed or anise seed
>   ¾ teaspoon ground cumin
>   A scant pinch of black pepper

Steep all the flavorings in vodka and follow directions as above.

Aquavit

Aqua vitae, which means "the water of life," is not really a liqueur but a caraway flavored drink popular in Norway. It is handy to use as an eau de vie to flavor other liqueurs that may need an added touch to give them a necessary kick.

>   1½ teaspoons slightly crushed caraway seed
>   1½ cups brandy or vodka

Let stand for 2 weeks. Strain and filter and it is ready to drink or use in food and cocktail recipes. No sweetener is added.
Yield: 1½ cups

LEMON BALM OR MELISSA

Lemon balm, or melissa, is a versatile herb with many uses. The leaf, which is used for the flavor, resembles mint, but the taste and aroma are more like lemon. The ancients thought of it as a symbol of sympathy and gentleness and termed it a cure-all. With this information, it is nice to know that melissa may be used in cold soups, hot cream soups, roast lamb, stuffings for pork or turkey, and in fruit and vegetable salads. The fresh leaf is very delicate and should be washed and chopped just before using as it tends to discolor. The dried leaf may be used for all flavorings and in making liqueurs without this problem.

The dried herb is available in health food stores. For fresh leaves, the plant is easy to grow in many climates. Use the fresh or dried leaf for making a liqueur and for adding flavor to other herb recipes or to citrus recipes that require lemon flavoring. Melissa is an excellent digestif, a welcome after-dinner drink as well as a delightful additive to your cooking-flavoring repertoire.

Melissa with vodka

2½ teaspoons dried melissa
Sliced and scraped peel of ¼ lemon
A pinch of coriander
A pinch of cinnamon
2 peppermint leaves
1 cup vodka
½ cup sugar syrup

Place all the ingredients in a bottle (including the sugar syrup) and steep 3 weeks. Shake the jar daily during the steeping period. Strain and filter into a dark bottle, adding more sugar to taste. Mature for 2 months.
Yield: 1½ cups

Melissa liqueur with brandy

> 2 tablespoons dried melissa
> Sliced peel of ¼ lemon
> 1½ cups brandy
> ½ cup sugar syrup

Steep the melissa and lemon peel in brandy for 2 days. Filter and sweeten. It's ready to drink, but will taste even better after several weeks.
Yield: 2 cups

MINT

When you price mint and peppermint cordials and compare them to the same amount of vodka, you'll run to your garden or condiment shelf and mix batches of the delicious liqueur. It is so refreshing served in a small glass, or poured over ice cream. And what a flavor it gives to packaged cake mixes! Use extracts or concentrates and you can mix it up now and have it to drink tomorrow. Fresh and dried mint leaves require a little longer.

Mint, peppermint and spearmint, are all in the same family and may be used interchangeably or combined in the following recipe. Add a drop of green food coloring for visual effect and see it sparkle when you hold it to the light in a clear glass.

Make a large recipe because you can also use it as the basis for chocolate mint, coconut mint, orange mint, or other flavor combinations that strike your fancy. Use it, too, in a hypodermic needle and plunge it deeply into chocolate covered cherry candies, into fresh strawberries and cherries. (See page 181.)

Mint liqueurs

> 12-14 tablespoons fresh or 6 teaspoons dried, well-crumpled mint, peppermint, or spearmint leaves OR 2-3 teaspoons pure mint or peppermint extract
> 3 cups vodka
> 1 teaspoon glycerine (optional) but nice for sipping
> 1 cup sugar syrup (for crème de menthe add 2 cups)

With fresh or dried leaves: steep the leaves in vodka for 10 days and shake the bottle occasionally. Strain and filter. Be sure to press all the juices from the leaves with a spoon against the strainer. Mature 2 weeks. With the extract: combine all ingredients. Shake well. Mature 24 hours minimum. A week or 2 will enhance the flavoring.

If any of these recipes results in too weak a mint flavor, add more of the extract or leaves and repeat the steeping, straining, and maturing procedures.

Should any globules of oil form on the surface of the liqueur, remove with a bit of blotting paper or paper toweling, dabbing them gently.

ROSEMARY

You'll find this herb has one of the nicest aromas for your liqueur making; it's like a mixed breed of sage and lavender, ginger and camphor, all grown in one attractive plant. Even if you don't know what the plant looks like, you'll appreciate what nature can create when you realize that the whole dried leaf or ground leaf can be used extensively in cooking.

Rosemary holds center stage in a fascinating series of folk beliefs; if someone was giddy, or had no sense of smell, the cure called for eating a loaf of bread that had been baked on a bed of rosemary. It was used as incense in religious ceremonies and placed in an amulet to ward against evil. Brides carried a sprig of rosemary in their bouquet for luck while widows tossed a sprig of it on the graves of their husbands.

Rosemary, as most herbs, was used extensively for medicinal purposes; when specifically prepared and taken internally it reputedly was good for gout. When a salve was applied to the skin, it relieved dermatological disorders.

For liqueur we suggest mixing a small recipe. Keep the amount of rosemary scant as it has strong flavoring ability.

Rosemary liqueur

> 1½ teaspoons rosemary leaves OR 1 teaspoon
>   ground rosemary
> 1 mint leaf
> Sliced and scraped peel of ½ lemon
> ¼ teaspoon coriander
> 1½ cups vodka
> ½ cup sugar syrup

Gently crush the rosemary leaves and mint with the back of a spoon on a breadboard so the aroma and oils are released. Add the lemon and herbs to the vodka and steep for 10 days. Strain and filter. Add the sugar syrup. Mature for 2–4 weeks.
Yield: 2 cups

SAGE

In ancient times, the rather common garden plant "sage" was the symbol of wisdom; thus wise men are called "sages." You'll be equally wise if you use the herb to make liqueurs. It is unfortunate that most people think of the flavoring only for use in turkey and chicken stuffings for it is delightful when it is blended into soft cheeses, rubbed onto the tops of roasts, and sprinkled on salads. It provides an unusual pungent, though slightly bitter, flavor that gives it character. As a liqueur, it may be combined with other flavors for a distinctive drink.

Sage is available in whole dried leaves, which can be broken or crushed, and in ground form. You may have the fresh sage growing in your garden and not be aware of it. The sage leaf is taken from a variety of salvia, specifically *salvia officinalis,* a perennial plant with violet-blue flowers that grows throughout the United States. The recipe combines the flavor with white wine and vodka and yields about 3¾ cups of finished liqueur. Divide all ingredients in half if you prefer.

Sage liqueur

> 12-14 fresh sage leaves OR 4 teaspoons dried OR 2
>   teaspoons ground sage
> 2 whole cloves
> Sliced and scraped peel of one lemon
> 1½ cups dry white wine
> 1¼ cups vodka
> 1 cup sugar syrup

Lightly crush the sage leaves, add the clove and lemon peel to the white wine and vodka for 2 weeks. Strain and filter; add the sugar syrup. Mature 4-8 weeks.

POTPOURRI

The history of liqueurs reveals that the early brews developed by the alchemists often contained an uncanny variety of rare and precious herbs and spices. John French, who wrote a seventeenth-century treatise on distillation in England, gave a recipe for liqueur named "Aqua Celestis." It contained 62 different herbs, spices, berries, nuts, fruits, flower petals, and leaves plus the alcohol and sweetener. More recent books present recipes with anywhere from 10–30 herbs. If one were to try to follow any of the recipes exactly, tracking down the exact herbs could be a 6-month project.

With these recipes as our cue we assembled a pinch of this and ¼ teaspoon of that, a few leaves from several different herbs, and a piece of scraped lemon peel, and some fruits. We placed it all into a quart jar with 3 cups of vodka. We let it steep for 2 weeks, strained and filtered it, then added the sugar syrup. Result? Amazingly delicious.

Potpourri recipe brewed by you

All the herbs and spices you like totaling about 3 tablespoons using a pinch of each such as cinnamon, nutmeg, and sage, a few seeds such as coriander, fennel, anise, and caraway and crumble 2 or 3 leaves such as mint, melissa, bay, or rosemary. Add a clove. Add the scraped peel of ¼ lemon, a few currants, ¼ piece of tangerine or orange to:

> 3 cups vodka OR half vodka and half brandy
> 1 cup sugar syrup

Steep the ingredients in the alcohol about 2 weeks. Filter and strain. Add the sugar syrup to taste.
Yield: about 4 cups

NOTE: Refer to the following chapter using nuts, beans, and other ingredients and do the same thing. Or add some of the nut flavorings to the above combination.

GROWING YOUR OWN HERBS AND SPICES

The herbs you need to make your own liqueurs can be as close as your kitchen window sill or backyard garden. Many can be grown in a variety of climates (some are so hearty they flourish in every climate). As you learn about the herbs we have suggested for the liqueurs, and refer to a garden book, you'll discover that many of them are used for ground cover, shrubs, and ornamental plantings.

Growing your own herbs is easy and there are several books available for the specialty gardener. Consult lists of plant names. You can quickly discover those used for seasoning, medicine, or liqueurs because they bear the species name *officinalis* (meaning: sold in shops, edible, medicinal, recognized in the pharmacopoeia). Briefly some you may try in various climates and landscape situations are:

Kitchen gardens

The following are ideal for a sunny herb garden near a kitchen door or in planter boxes for your window: mint, rosemary, sage, thyme, angelica, anise, caraway, coriander, and common fennel.

Ground covers

In sunny areas, plant prostrate rosemary, which creeps among rocks and has a delectable aroma, and caraway scented thyme.

Perennial or shrub borders and hedges

Common wormwood, lavenders, rosemary, scented geraniums, sage (salvia), hyssop, thyme.

Rock gardens

Sage, wooly thyme, winter savory.

Moist areas

Angelica, mint, parsley, lemon balm.

Drying herbs

Use some of the herbs fresh, and dry some of them for cooking. Leafy herbs should be cut early in the day before the sun is too hot but after the dew is dry and when the oil content is highest. Sage should be cut early in the summer. Other leafy herbs are ready from the time flower buds begin to form until the flowers are half open. Plan to cut 2–3 crops of herbs during the growing season but don't cut perennial herbs after September.

Sort the herbs from any weeds or grass and remove dead or insect damaged leaves. Wash off in cool water and shake or blot excess moisture.

Woody stemmed herbs should be tied by the stems in small bundles and hung upside down from a line hung across a dark, but airy room about 70° temperature. If the room is not dark, use a paper clip to hold a cylinder of dark paper around the bunch.

Large leafed herbs, such as basil, that do not bundle easily to allow air to circulate around them, should be dried flat. Prepare a piece of screening or a tray with holes. Cover the screen or tray with cheesecloth or paper toweling. Lay a single layer of leaves on top of the cloth or toweling, and move them around a little each day. Store in a dark airy room.

Herbs should dry in a few days to 1 week. Strip leaves from stems, crumble, store in glass jars, and label them with the name of the herb and the date.

Seed herbs

Gather seed clusters from anise, fennel, caraway, and coriander when they turn brown. Seeds should begin to fall off the clusters when the cluster is gently tapped. Collect each type of seed in a separate box and knock the seeds from the clusters; spread the seeds in the box and leave in the sun to dry (throw away the clusters). When partially dry, separate any chaff from the seeds and dry about 2 more weeks in the sun. Store as for leafy herbs.

6

Beans, Nuts, Flowers, Eggs, and Teas

Several aperitifs and after-dinner drinks that are usually considered liqueurs defy classification among the citrus fruit, herb, and spice recipes. They are made from a variety of beans such as cacao and vanilla, nuts, flower petals, eggs, and tea. Chocolate and coffee flavored alcoholic drinks have so escalated in popularity that an entire market of offshoot products has been developed.

Many of these delicious drinks can be simulated using the same maceration methods described in the previous chapters. The alcoholic content can be raised or lowered by altering the amount of water added.

The following recipes emphasize the use of a flavoring ingredient for the dominant taste. Always think about other ingredients that might be added.

Always buy the best and freshest quality flavorings you can. If you use flower petals, try those you grow yourself and avoid spraying them with insecticides.

COFFEE

The Mexican "Kahlua" and Jamaican "Tia Maria" are probably the best known coffee flavored liqueurs. Other companies produce similar drinks called Moka, Mocha, Crème de Mocha, and so forth. Coffee is among the easiest flavors to simulate. We received many recipes from our friends that varied only slightly from one another. It seemed that everyone had made a version of "Kahlua" at one time and treasured his own recipe.

Coffee-vodka

2 cups water
2 cups white sugar
½ cup dry instant coffee (fresh jar)
½ chopped vanilla bean
1½ cups vodka
Caramel coloring (optional)

Boil water and sugar until dissolved. Turn off heat. Slowly add dry instant coffee and continue stirring. Add a chopped vanilla bean to the vodka, then combine the cooled sugar syrup and coffee solution with the vodka. Cover tightly and shake vigorously each day for 3 weeks. Strain and filter.
Yield: about 4 cups

Coffee-rum

Substitute rum for the vodka to yield simulated Tia Maria. Substitute brandy for the vodka for another simulated Kahlua drink.

Optional flavorings: a pinch of cinnamon, cloves, orange peel, cardamom, mint.

Food colorings, flavor extracts, and spices already on your kitchen shelf are perfect for flavoring liqueurs.

VANILLA

Vanilla, usually associated with ice cream and puddings, will blend well with alcohol to make a delicious liqueur though it has not caught on commercially. It is frequently used in conjunction with other flavorings and especially with cacao beans for the always popular

Crème de Cacao. A recent new flavor is Carmella, a combination of caramel and vanilla.

The plant from which vanilla is derived has an exotic background; the long cigar-like vanilla bean is the unripe fruit of an orchid bearing plant native to Mexico. It was brought to Europe by the Spanish Conquistadors but today the plants that yield the best vanilla are on Island of Reunion, near Madagascar.

Fresh vanilla beans are available in health food and gourmet shops, sold in long glass tubes or folded over in jars. The fresh bean has a smooth dark covering and may be about 8″ long with a soft lining that carries the flavor. When you open the tube the scent is enough to make a vanilla lover go crazy. A "stale" bean or one that has been on the shelf too long looks like a piece of dried beef and has shrunk to about half the size; the vanilla smell is stale. Pure vanilla extract may be substituted when making liqueurs.

Vanilla bean

> 2 fresh whole vanilla beans about 5″ long
> 1½ cups vodka
> ½ cup sugar syrup

Steep the vanilla beans in vodka and be sure they are immersed. Shake well and steep 2-3 weeks. Remove the beans and filter if necessary. Add the sugar syrup. Mature about 1 month.
Yield: 2 cups

Vanilla extract

> 1½ teaspoons pure vanilla extract, dried or ground vanilla
> 1 pinch cinnamon
> 1½ cups vodka or brandy
> ½ cup sugar syrup

Mix the vanilla and alcohol and shake well. Steep 1 week. Add the sugar syrup to the solution with the vanilla extract; no straining will be required. The dried or ground vanilla should be filtered before adding the sugar syrup. Mature at least 1 week.

Yield: 2 cups

CHOCOLATE

New chocolate blends of liqueur pop up in advertisements and stores every year. There are combinations of chocolate coconut, chocolate mint, chocolate cherry, chocolate strawberry, and recently the chocolate-cows, a milky chocolate liqueur drink with a low alcohol content. A Swiss liqueur, Marmot Chocolate, actually has pieces of chocolate in it.

Chocolate liqueurs are usually a blend of the cocoa bean with a proportion of vanilla pods. Interestingly, the distillation of the cocoa bean is not the brown we are accustomed to as chocolate, but a clear liquid which is colored in the production process.

The uses for chocolate liqueurs are as vast as the flavoring itself and you'll find several recipes for them in the second part of this book.

Homemade chocolate liqueurs and blends do not seem as rich bodied as those made commercially, such as Vandermint and Cherry Suisse, but they are an adequate substitute and much less costly. In addition to pure chocolate liqueur we have simulated blends such as chocolate-mint in the steeping process. We have also mixed two or three finished liqueurs together for our blends such as chocolate-orange but they must mature for a couple of weeks before the flavors are detectable and delectable.

> 2 teaspoons pure chocolate extract used for baking
> ½ teaspoon pure vanilla extract
> 1½ cups vodka
> ½ cup sugar syrup

Mix all the ingredients together and let mature several days.

Chocolate liqueurs may also be made with chocolate syrup and powdered cocoa but the flavor is not as strong and the solution forms a residue in the bottle which is unappetizing.

NUTS

A variety of nuts can be adapted to pleasant tasting, delicately aromatic liqueurs. We offer 5 flavors we have made which we consider successful and easy to duplicate. Try your favorites steeped in vodka or brandy. Add a trace of other compatible flavorings. Steep and sweeten. You may not perplex your tasters with the bouquet, but you may confound them with your inventiveness when you try such unlikely liqueurs as peanut, black walnut, or pistachio. You'll also discover such nut liqueurs as Kola, which is a Hawaiian blend of kola nuts, tonka beans, vanilla, and citrus peels. Nocino, Brou and Eau de Noix, are made by macerating walnut husks and herbs in brandy.

ALMOND

Probably the most popular nut flavor liqueur is almond and several companies market an amaretto liqueur under a variety of labels. Amaretto actually is produced from apricot nuts within the pits which have a strong bitter-almond flavor and not from almonds. According to historians, the distillation of apricot pits to produce amaretto was discovered in the fifteenth century. *Amaretto* is a generic term; "Amaretto di Saronna" is the trademark of a well-known brand, made in Italy. The name "Amaretto" is derived from the "amaretti" which are the local cookies or cakes that are made with crushed almonds.

Almond liqueurs made in the United States are usually processed from extracts or almond oil and labeled crème de almond. A newcomer to the market is the Mexican "Cuervo Almondrado," a blend of tequila and almonds.

You can simulate the almond flavor using extracts or concentrates. You can also make them from chopped fresh almonds. Try any or all of the following recipes, then improvise to create your own brand label and flavoring. The filtered nutmeats are a delicious addition to the "Fruitueur's Fantasy."

Almond liqueur with extract

> ½ teaspoon pure almond extract
> 1½ cups vodka
> ½ cup sugar syrup

Make the sugar syrup, cool it, add all the ingredients together, shake well. Mature a few days and it is ready to drink.
Yield: 2 cups

Chopped almond liqueur

Select fresh natural (unblanched and unsalted) almonds and chop them coarsely with a knife in a nut chopper. Chopping releases the flavorful oils. Do not chop them too fine or it will be difficult to filter.

> 3 ounces chopped, fresh (unblanched and unsalted)
>   almonds
> Pinch of cinnamon
> 1½ cups vodka
> ½ cup sugar syrup

Combine all ingredients, shake well, and steep about 2 weeks. Filter. Sweeten. Mature a few more weeks and it is ready to drink.
Yield: 2 cups

COCONUT

Anyone who has traveled to the Caribbean Islands is familiar with the many faces of the coconut in recipes from literally soup to nuts. In recent years coconut has become extremely popular as a liqueur by itself and in combination with other flavors and with different alcohol bases. CocoRibe is a combination of coconut and rum. We like the coconut by itself. Try it mixed with orange or vanilla too.

Fresh coconut

> 12 ounces of fresh coconut, the white meaty
>   portion
> 3 coriander seeds
> 1″ piece of vanilla bean or a drop of vanilla extract
> 10 ounces vodka
> 3 ounces brandy

Cut the coconut meat into small pieces or grate on a large grater and add all the ingredients in a bottle. Steep 3 weeks and shake it gently every 3-4 days. Strain and filter. Sugar syrup may not be required but if it is, add 1-2 ounces at a time rather than by ½ cups. Coconut has an unusually large amount of natural sugar. Yield: About 2 cups

PEANUT

We have indicated that the commercial producers must continually offer new tastes, new combinations to inject spirit into the monetary aspects of liqueurs. Each year, researchers doggedly delve into every possible combination to develop blends that will entice the public. Each company must keep this research secret so that competitors will not have a hint of what is going on, lest they should discover the marketable combination first.

So it was predictable that, in 1976, when Jimmy Carter became President of the United States his association with the peanut industry would inspire a peanut liqueur. We jumped on the same bandwagon and produced our own peanut liqueur. It was an instant success to those who swoon over peanut butter, peanut candies, peanut bars, and plain peanuts. We have combined peanuts with chocolate and raisins—simulations of our personal taste fetishes. For a downright decadent adventure, we offer our concoction:

Peanut liqueur

> 4 ounces fresh unsalted, unroasted peanuts, shelled
> 3" piece of vanilla bean (or ¼ teaspoon vanilla extract)
> 1½ cups vodka
> ½ cup sugar syrup

Chop the peanuts slightly and, with the vanilla, add to the vodka. Steep 2 weeks. Strain and filter. Add sugar syrup and mature 2 months.
Yield: 2 cups

PISTACHIO AND WALNUT

All nut recipes are made the same way. Only the type of nut and the added flavorings create different tastes. If you are unsure about flavorings that go well with a certain nut, refer to cookbooks for cookies and dessert recipes. For example, if you wonder what spices to add to a walnut liqueur, look up walnut in the index of a cookbook and note recipes such as walnut cheese pie or spice walnut raisin pie. One calls for vanilla, another calls for cinnamon, cloves, and raisins. This is your cue that any of the above can be added successfully to the liqueur for flavoring.

3-4 ounces of chopped black walnuts or pistachio
    nuts
Pinch of cinnamon
Pinch of cloves
12 raisins or currants (optional)
1½ cups vodka
½ cup sugar syrup

Steep the nuts, raisins, and spices in vodka for 2 weeks.
Shake occasionally. Strain and filter. Add the sugar
syrup. Mature 2-3 weeks.
Yield: about 2-2½ cups

EGG LIQUEUR

Liqueurs made from eggs are a European delight. So
popular are they that housewives often make the liqueur
to use in baking and cooking. Advockaat is a thick
sweet egg and brandy emulsion which sometimes has to
be eaten with a spoon.

The following egg liqueur recipe was offered to us by
one of our correspondents, Peggy Moulton, who
gleaned it from a European housewife. We have had to
experiment and revise the original recipe slightly to use
the ingredients available. It's delicious by itself, in
baking recipes and added to eggnog.

Egg liqueur

    8 egg yolks
    2 drops vanilla extract
    1 cup sugar
    1 large (15 ounces) can condensed milk
    20 ounces brandy OR ⅔ brandy, ⅓ vodka

Beat the egg yolks, vanilla, and sugar until pale lemon colored at medium speed in a mixer or by hand beater. While beating add the milk slowly. Add the alcohol and stir thoroughly. Put in a tightly covered bottle and store in a cool, dark place unopened for a year. After opening, the shelf life is about 5 months when kept in a cool place. (Ours was consumed before that time so we can't vouch for the shelf life.)
Yield: about 4½ cups

Eggs with Marsala wine

Another European recipe results in a rich, creamy liqueur that tastes like the filling of Italian pastries. It makes an excellent sauce for cream puffs, ice cream, and cakes.

    5 egg yolks
    1 cup milk
    1½ cups sugar
    1 cup dry Marsala wine
    ½ teaspoon vanilla extract
    8 ounces vodka or brandy

Beat the egg yolks and add to the sugar in a double boiler or non-stick pan. Slowly add the milk, the vanilla, and ½ of the wine. Heat and stir as the mixture thickens to remove any lumps. Bring to a boil slowly and simmer for 5 minutes, stirring it to prevent scorching. Remove the mixture from the stove and stir while cooling. Add the remainder of the wine and all the alcohol. Pour into a bottle and seal tightly, shake it well, let it mature about 6 weeks, then it is ready for drinking.

Yield: 4 to 5 cups

FLOWER PETALS

Nearly every old cookbook from England, Italy, and France has recipes for spirits made with flower petals. Today, we most likely associate aromas such as lavender, rosehips, carnations, jasmine, and cherry blossom with other products: teas, perfumes, sachets, colognes. Commercially, liqueurs made with flowers have become almost obsolete. The do-it-yourself liqueur maker who can use fresh flowers plucked from his garden can discover a never ending source of experimentation, excitement, satisfaction . . . and economy.

The not-so-green thumb liqueur maker can purchase fresh flowers from a nursery or florist. Many dried flower petals are available from health food stores or sources specializing in herbs and spices listed in the Appendix. Look for carnations, hibiscus, lavender, marigold, orange, jasmine, and rosehips.

Prepare fresh flower petals by cutting the heads of the flowers when they are in full bloom. Separate the petals from the stamen and stems. Gently wash and pat them dry.

Steep the flower petals in vodka. Strain. Add sweetener, using the same procedures outlined in Chapter 2. Additional spices may be used. Some of the herb liqueurs can be combined with the flower petal recipes to perk up and alter a taste. Generally for a 2-2½-cup yield you will need:

1½ cups fresh petals OR ⅓ cup dried petals

Fresh flower petals

> 1½ cups highly scented fresh petals, washed and dabbed dry on paper towels
> 1½ cups vodka
> ½ cup sugar syrup

Steep the petals in vodka 2-3 weeks. Strain and squeeze out the juices. Add sugar syrup. Mature approximately 1 week.

Try several varieties of petals in one brew for a "floribunda" flavor.

Dried flower petals

> 2-3 tablespoons dried flower petals
> 1½ cups vodka
> ½ cup sugar

Follow the same procedure as above.
Yield: 2 cups (16 ounces)

Optional flavorings: cardamom, caraway, lemon peel, orange peel.

Petals strained from the liqueur may be used for brewing teas.

TEAS

Tea liqueurs are not so popular as coffee liqueurs, but if you're a tea drinker and want to try a divine flavor, we suggest black tea liqueur. We made it and mentioned it to someone who told us she had bought a bottle of it commercially produced in Florida. We haven't found it in our part of the country yet. Our congratulations to whoever decided it's a worthwhile flavor, for our tasters consistently voted it among the top ten. Certainly it's among the easiest to make.

The only variance in making tea liqueurs from other herb and leaf-like plants is that the steeping time must be reduced to not more than 24 hours or the bitter taste from the tannin in the tea will permeate your liqueur.

Consider tea liqueur flavors much as you would teas alone. A survey of flavors in any gourmet shop will reveal a wide variety of blends, all adaptable to liqueurs and your taste preferences.

Add flavorings such as orange peel, cloves, cinnamon, cardamom, and try honey for sweetener in place of sugar syrup.

Tea leaves

2 teaspoons black tea leaves (or other)
1½ cups vodka or brandy
½ cup sugar syrup

Steep tea in alcohol 24 hours. *No longer.* Strain. Add sweetener to taste. Mature 1 week.
Yield: 2 cups

Part 2
Cooking with
Liqueurs

7

A Casual, Gourmet Cook

Making liqueurs can be habit forming. Drinking them can, too, though we hope, not in excessive quantities. Liqueurs are so easy to make, you may have a cabinet full of exotic flavors before you realize what you have concocted.

What will you do with all of them?

Test them, sip them, serve them. Give them for gifts, of course.

Cook with them.

Lemon-lime, apricot, and raspberry brandy liqueurs steep. Glazed Cornish hens (page 149) and Pineapple-shrimp boats (page 128) are as pleasing to look at as they are to taste.
Pages 114 and 115:
Turkey with orange liqueur basting sauce; dressing made with corn bread and plum liqueur; yams made with pineapple liqueur; blueberry muffins made with banana liqueur; dessert made with pistachio-mint pudding and black walnut liqueur using the "Fruitueur's Fantasy" in the pudding.

Yes. Using the liqueurs you make in the foods you cook can elevate basic recipes into the gourmet category. That extra touch of flavoring in soups, appetizers, sauces for roasts, and salad dressings, as well as desserts and drinks, will bring oohs, ahhs, and compliments to the most casual chefs.

It's so easy to be inspired, too, and creative. With a little logic, you can quickly comprehend how to use the liqueurs advantageously and with flair for flavoring. Most liqueurs are blends of fruits, herbs, and spices, all used in cooking. By adding liqueurs with flavorings similar to condiments called for in recipes, the dish will have extra zip and zest.

The only caution is not to overdo or to use a liqueur that might seem incompatible with the food you are making. For instance, a chocolate liqueur used to flavor a ham sauce doesn't seem quite right while an orange or pineapple sauce would be the more complementary flavor.

When you are using commercial liqueurs and you are not sure of the basic flavoring, check the liqueur list on pages 33-35.

A few things to remember about liqueurs will help you be successful every time you use them:

- Always add liqueurs with moderation; try a drop or two at a time and taste the recipe as you go when possible.
- When you are pleased with the amount of liqueur added to a recipe, note how much you added; the next time you can repeat the taste.
- When liqueur is added to a recipe that must be heated, the alcohol will evaporate and only the flavoring will remain. When possible, add the liqueur just before serving and the flavor will be stronger.
- When foods are stored in a refrigerator or freezer for a few days or a week and must be reheated or recooked, add the liqueur again if taste tells you it has dissipated.
- Do not store liqueurs in plastic containers or seal with plastic covers.
- The same recipe with the same flavor liqueur can vary when different brands or types of liqueurs are used. Orange liqueurs, for example, made with fruits from different parts of the world will vary. Your homemade orange liqueurs may differ if the oranges are of different varieties. The taste difference may not be significant, but it may be noticeable.

How to flambé

Flambé, or flaming, is a spectacular service for fruits, crêpes, pancakes, and sauces. The procedure can be used for any meal; brunch, lunch, dinner, or whenever the mood moves you. High drama occurs when the flames dance decorously from pans with room lights dimmed or late at night. It's like a moving miniature fireplace for a few minutes while the flames lick up into the air.

It's all accomplished with a high proof, flavored alcohol added to a sweetened pan of warm foods and lit with a match. The alcohol is the flaming agent and the flavor remains in the dish. See the flambé recipes on page 144, 162, 185, 186.

Here's all you need to know for successful flambé dishes:

Both sugar and alcohol are required for flaming. Both should be warmed to at least 75° or you may not get any effect at all.

1. Warm the food in a covered chafing dish or a skillet.

2. Warm the alcohol in a pan or a pitcher but do not let it boil. 100-proof alcohol may ignite at about room temperature. A lower proof liqueur (40, 60-80) should be heated to about 160°-180°. Gourmet shops sell flavored, 175-proof flambé products.

3. Sprinkle sugar over the food, pour the warmed liqueur over the sugar, cover the pan for a minute,

then remove the cover and hold a lit match over the food until it ignites. Stand back and enjoy.

4. To keep the flame going and the food warm, carefully float additional liqueur on top of the food and re-ignite as necessary. Long matches used to light fireplaces are ideal for flambéing.

WARNING: Never pour alcohol directly from the bottle onto hot food when flambéing. The fire may ignite the alcohol all the way up to the bottle and cause a ball of fire to form which can shoot out and ignite clothing, curtains, and so forth.

8

Artful Appetizers

Blue cheese spread

½ pound blue cheese, softened
½ pound unsalted butter or margarine, softened
¼ cup *apricot liqueur* or *cassis liqueur*
¼ cup chopped walnuts, chopped coarsely

Beat cheese and butter until creamy. Beat in liqueur and stir in nuts. Chill. Serve spread with thin sliced rye, pumpernickel, or crackers.
Yield: 2 cups

A walnut-liqueur flavored cheese log and an allspice liqueur dip. Photo courtesy Diamond Walnut Growers, Inc., Stockton, CA.

Sweet and sour meatballs

> 2 pounds ground roundsteak
> 2 pieces white bread, crusts removed, soaked in
>   cold water and then the water squeezed out
> 1 egg, beaten
> 1 teaspoon salt
> ¼ teaspoon pepper
> 1 8-ounce jar grape jelly
> ¾ cup catsup mixed with ¼ cup water
> 1 tablespoon sugar
> ¼ cup lemon juice
> 2 tablespoons white vinegar
> ¾ cup raisins
> ¼ cup *berry liqueur*

Mix ground steak, squeezed out bread, egg, salt, and pepper. Form into small meatballs (cocktail size) and brown lightly. Add jelly, catsup with water, sugar, lemon juice, vinegar and simmer 2 hours. Add raisins and liqueur during last ½ hour. Serve hot.

When preparing ahead of time and refrigerating or freezing, cook 1½ hours. Then add raisins and liqueur when reheating just before serving.
Yield: about 30 meatballs for 6–8 people

Fruity shrimp dip

> 1 cup cooked shrimp, finely chopped
> 3 ounces cream cheese
> ½ cup pineapple yogurt
> 1 ounce *orange liqueur*

Blend all ingredients together well. Chill.
Yield: 1¾ cups

Oriental dip

    1 9-ounce jar chutney
    ½ cup *cranberry liqueur*
    2 tablespoons *orange liqueur* or *tangerine liqueur*
    ¼ cup water

Blend all ingredients in blender or food processor until smooth. Pour into 2-quart saucepan. Simmer and stir 5 minutes until dipping consistency. A perfect dip for hot fried shrimp and egg rolls.
Yield: 2 cups

Ham rolls

    1½ pounds ham, thinly sliced
    6 ounces red currant jelly
    1 tablespoon *cherry liqueur*
    1 teaspoon chopped onion
    ¼ teaspoon dry mustard
    ½ teaspoon ground ginger
    ½ teaspoon grated lemon rind

Roll ham slices, secure with wooden picks. Melt jelly in chafing dish, add remaining ingredients, and heat. Heat ham rolls in this sauce and serve.
Yield: 15-20 appetizers

Allspice liqueur dip

    8 ounces sour cream
    1 package onion or mushroom dried soup mix
    2 teaspoons *allspice liqueur*

Blend all ingredients together well. Chill.
Yield: 1 cup

Herbed liver pâté

1 pound chicken livers
1 onion chopped
½ teaspoon salt
¼ teaspoon pepper
¼ cup shortening or creamed butter
1 tablespoon *potpourri herb liqueur*
1 hard-cooked egg

Broil chicken livers and onions until livers are brown. Chop in blender or food processor. Add salt, pepper, shortening, and liqueur while livers remain warm. Blend well. Place in bowl and refrigerate. Invert bowl on platter when ready to serve and remove bowl. Garnish liver with hard-cooked egg pressed through a strainer. Serve with cocktail crackers or rye rounds. Yield: 1½ cups

Cheddar cheese spread

8 ounces soft or grated cheddar cheese
3 ounces cream cheese
8 ounces small curd cottage cheese
1 tablespoon orange rind
3 ounces *orange liqueur* or *apricot liqueur*
½ cup crushed almonds or pecans

Put cottage cheese through a sieve. Mix cheddar and cream cheese together until smooth, then add to cottage cheese. Stir in liqueur and orange rind. Add nuts and stir until smooth. Place in serving bowl and let stand for at least an hour, or make well before serving and refrigerate. Serve at room temperature. Yield: 2½ cups

Orange rumaki

> ½ pound chicken livers
> 3 tablespoons *orange liqueur*
> 1 clove garlic, chopped
> ⅓ cup soy sauce
> 1 small can water chestnuts, drained
> ½ pound bacon slices, halved

Marinate chicken livers in orange liqueur, garlic, and soy sauce for 1 hour. Combine chestnut with piece of liver and wrap with bacon, secure with toothpick. Bake in 400° oven till bacon is crisp.

Walnut cheese logs

> 1 pound soft cheddar cheese
> 2 3-ounce packages cream cheese
> ¼ pound blue cheese
> ¼ pound smoked cheese
> 1 tablespoon prepared mustard
> 1 teaspoon grated onion
> 1 tablespoon *walnut liqueur*
> 2 tablespoons Port wine
> Cream
> 1 cup chopped walnuts

Grate cheddar cheese; combine with one package of cream cheese, blue cheese, and smoked cheese. Mix in mustard, grated onion, liqueur, and wine, using either an electric mixer or your hands. Shape into logs about an inch in diameter. Blend remaining package of cream cheese with enough cream until of spreading consistency and spread over the logs. Roll in walnuts. Wrap in aluminum foil and chill in refrigerator. Slice and serve on assorted crackers.
Yield: 24 servings

Anise peanuts

½ cup *anise liqueur* (or *fennel* or *licorice*)
½ teaspoon garlic powder
¼ teaspoon curry powder
2 cups unroasted skinless peanuts
1 tablespoon vegetable oil
½ teaspoon salt

Spread the liqueur in a shallow oiled roasting pan, add garlic and curry powder, then peanuts. Mix. Sprinkle with salt. Bake at 300° for 10 minutes, stirring once. Serve.
Yield: 2 cups

Pineapple-shrimp boat

1½ cups Thousand Island salad dressing
2 ounces *orange liqueur* or *lemon-lime liqueur*
1 fresh pineapple
1 pound small cooked shrimp

Stir the liqueur into the dressing. Cut pineapple in half, remove fruit carefully with a grapefruit knife. Cut into ½″ cubes, using about ¾ of the fruit. Add shrimp to pineapple and place loosely into scooped out pineapple halves. Pour sauce over fruit and shrimp. Place pineapple on platter and serve with toothpicks.
Yield: 8-10 servings

Chicken spread

1 cup chicken spread (two 4-ounce cans)
8 ounces cream cheese, softened
½ teaspoon salt
¼ teaspoon pepper
2 teaspoons *allspice liqueur*
1 teaspoon *anise liqueur*
10 pimiento-stuffed olives

Mix all ingredients together thoroughly until blended. Place in a shaped bowl or mold pan and chill. Invert on a serving platter with lettuce leaves. Decorate with sliced pimiento olives. Serve with crackers.
Yield: 2 cups

Caraway cashews

    2 cups uncooked cashews
    2 tablespoons melted butter
    1 tablespoon vegetable oil
    1 tablespoon *caraway liqueur*
    ½ teaspoon salt
    ½ teaspoon paprika
    ¼ teaspoon ground cumin seed

Mix nuts, butter, oil, and liqueur in a shallow roasting pan. Bake at 350° for 20–25 minutes or until nuts are light brown in color. Shake pan frequently and stir nuts; drain on paper towel. Mix salt, paprika, and cumin seed and sprinkle over nuts.
Yield: 2 cups

Fresh fruit appetizers

Serve any in-season fruits; add a few teaspoons of a *fruit liqueur, nut liqueur,* or *mint liqueur* gently mixed through. Marinate canned or fresh pineapple cubes in *crème de menthe.* Serve in a stemmed glass with finely chopped fresh mint and a few mint leaves for garnish.

9

Devilish Drinks

Fabulous drinks to be served before, during, and after dinner can be made with liqueurs. In the following recipes, observe the flavor combinations and feel free to improvise. For example, the traditional recipe for a Black Russian calls for equal parts coffee liqueur and vodka. Try your own variation! Instead of all coffee, use part coffee and part chocolate and give the drink a new name.

A recipe that calls for orange may be equally good with apricot or peach liqueur. Generally, the purpose for adding a dry spirit such as vodka or brandy is to cut the sweetness.

When a "color" liqueur is specified, such as white crème de menthe, it is generally for esthetic reasons, not flavor, so a green may be used.

Any of these devilish drinks can be served in any glass.

When mixing drinks that are to be *stirred* put ice in the glass first. When mixing *shake* drinks, add ice last. Drinks that are to be *blended* usually call for crushed ice.

For additional recipes refer to bartender books. The following recipes yield one serving. A jigger equals 1½ ounces.

Café cherry

> 1½ ounces *cherry liqueur*
> 1 teaspoon sugar
> 3 ounces cold coffee
> 1 egg white

Shake well with ice and strain into glass.

Café Mexican

> 1 ounce *coffee liqueur*
> 1 teaspoon sugar
> Dash of powdered cloves
> 1 cup strong black coffee
> Cinnamon stick

Add coffee to liqueur, sugar, and cloves in a mug or heated glass. Stir with cinnamon stick.

Snowball

> 2 ounces *thick egg liqueur*
> Dash of lime

Add sparkling lemonade or lemon-lime mixers to taste.

Breakfast eggnog

¼ ounce *orange liqueur*
1 fresh egg
¾ ounce brandy
¼ ounce milk
Nutmeg

Shake well with ice and strain into glass. Sprinkle grated nutmeg on top.

Black Russian

1½ ounces *coffee liqueur*
1½ ounces vodka

Stir and serve on the rocks.

Grasshopper

1 ounce *green mint* or *crème de menthe*
1 ounce *white crème de cacao*
1 ounce cream
½ cup crushed ice

Shake all together or put in a blender. Strain and serve.

Third rail

1–2 dashes *orange liqueur*
1–2 dashes *crème de menthe*
2–3 ounces dry vermouth
2–3 ice cubes
Twist lemon peel

Combine all ingredients except peel in a mixing glass and stir well. Strain into a cocktail glass and serve with lemon twist.

Kir

> 6 ounces dry white wine
> 1 tablespoon *crème de cassis*
> 2 or 3 ice cubes
> Twist of lemon peel

Combine all ingredients except the lemon peel in a goblet or wine glass. Stir gently. Twist lemon peel to release oil, then drop peel into the glass.

Sidecar

> ½ ounce *orange liqueur*
> 2 ounces brandy
> ½ ounce lemon juice
> 3-4 ice cubes

Combine all ingredients in a cocktail shaker and shake well. Strain into a cocktail glass.

Sombrero

> 2 ounces *coffee liqueur*
> Dash of light cream

Pour liqueur over ice; lighten with cream and stir lightly.

Frappés

Frappés may be made in any of three ways using any liqueur or compatible combination of liqueurs.

1. Pour liqueur over shaved ice heaped in a cocktail glass. Serve with a straw.
2. Fill a shaker ½ full with shaved ice; add liqueur, shake thoroughly and strain into a glass.
3. Blend ice and liqueur together in a blender and pour unstrained into a glass.

Orange-apricot delight frappé

1½ ounces *orange liqueur*
1½ ounces *apricot liqueur*

Shake well with crushed ice and strain into a glass.

Caraway-blackberry frappé

½ ounce *caraway* (Kümmel) *liqueur*
2 teaspoons blackberry brandy

Combine without ice. Stir well. Strain over crushed ice.

Mixed mocha frappé

¾ ounce *coffee liqueur*
1 teaspoon *white crème de menthe*
1 teaspoon *white crème de cacao*
1 teaspoon *orange liqueur*

Combine with ice and stir. Dip the rum, rubbed with lemon juice, into sugar to frost. Pour over crushed ice.

Pousse café

A book about liqueurs would be incomplete without a recipe for this spectacular drink. It consists of several different colored liqueurs floating on top of one another. The secret that prevents the liquids from mixing is the specific gravity of each; sweeter liqueurs are heavier and are placed in the glass first; they support drier, lighter weight liqueurs or brandy. Generally—but not always—the higher the proof the lighter the liqueur. A pousse café is not easy to make, especially with homemade liqueurs (even the same liqueur by different companies differs in specific gravity), but it's fun to try. Always keep a record of those that are used so you know which will work. To float one liqueur on another hold the bowl of the teaspoon face down over the drink and slowly pour each flavor over the back of the spoon. Or pour each new flavor slowly down the side of a tilted glass.

Angel's delight pousse café

¼ ounce *cherry liqueur*
¼ ounce *green crème de menthe liqueur*
¼ ounce *orange liqueur*
¼ ounce heavy cream

The progression is based on specific gravities of commercial liqueurs. When using those you make, if you are not sure one flavor will support, or float on top of another, test the two in a small glass before adding to the entire array. Mix these in a tall parfait or tulip champagne glass.

It is possible to intensify colors with a touch of food coloring. Try color combinations that tie in with a holiday such as green and red for Christmas; red, white, and blue for patriotic events; school colors for football games and reunion parties. Much of the drama is showing off your ability to create a pousse café for guests, so practice before you perform.

Stars and stripes pousse café

    ¼ ounce *crème de cassis liqueur*
    ¼ ounce *green chartreuse liqueur*
    ¼ ounce *maraschino cherry liqueur*

Proceed as with Angel's delight.

10

Elegant Entrées - Meat

Oriental kebabs

    1½ pounds sirloin or tenderloin steak, cubed
    2 cups fresh or canned pineapple, cubed
    2 green peppers, cut in 1″ cubes
    ½ pound fresh mushrooms
    4-6 cherry tomatoes

Marinade:
    ½ cup soy sauce
    ¼ cup brown sugar
    ½ teaspoon salt
    2 tablespoons lemon juice
    1 teaspoon *ginger liqueur*
    1 clove garlic, minced
    1 tablespoon salad oil

Combine marinade ingredients. Marinate meat 3-4 hours, turning occasionally. Alternate meat, pineapple, and assorted vegetables on skewers, ending each with a cherry tomato. Barbecue 2″-4″ from coals, basting with marinade as kebabs are turned.
Yield: 4 servings

Spear-it beef kabobs

Angelica pot roast

¾ cup dried prunes, pitted
¾ cup dried apricots
¾ cup raisins
1 cup *angelica liqueur*
2 tablespoons shortening
1 4-pound chuck roast
1 large onion, thinly sliced
3 tablespoons brown sugar
¼ cup honey
¼ cup water
½ teaspoon *cinnamon liqueur*
⅛ teaspoon *ginger liqueur*

Soak dried fruits in angelica liqueur overnight. Heat oil in skillet and brown meat on all sides. Add remaining ingredients, except fruit and liqueurs. Simmer over low flame or 300° oven for 2½ hours. Add fruit and cook ½ hour longer. Flavor with the liqueurs.

Pork chops with peaches

⅓ cup flour
½ teaspoon salt
¼ teaspoon pepper
⅛ teaspoon thyme
6 loin pork chops
2 tablespoons oil
1 can (16 ounces) sliced peaches, drained
¼ cup *apricot liqueur,* or *almond liqueur*

Combine flour, salt, pepper, and thyme. Dip pork chops in mixture, coating both sides. Heat oil in large skillet, brown chops. Cover and simmer 20 minutes. Add peaches and liqueur. Simmer covered an additional 20 minutes or until meat is tender.
Yield: 6 servings

Peachy lamb chops

    4 lamb chops, 1" thick
    ½ cup soy sauce
    ⅓ cup peach syrup
    3 tablespoons *peach liqueur*
    ½ teaspoon *ginger liqueur*
    1 clove garlic, minced
    4 canned peach halves

Marinate chops for several hours in a combination of soy sauce, peach syrup, liqueurs, and garlic. Remove chops and broil for 10 minutes on one side. Turn, place peaches on rack with chops. Brush chops with remaining marinade and broil.

Hungarian goulash

    1 blade chuck roast, 3–4 pounds, cubed
    ¼ cup seasoned flour
    ¼ oil
    ¼ cup stick margarine or butter
    3 pounds onions, sliced
    1 24-ounce can whole peeled tomatoes
    2½ tablespoons paprika
    1 teaspoon *caraway liqueur*
    Salt and pepper
    1 cup sour cream

Dredge meat in flour. Heat oil in heavy skillet. Brown meat well on all sides, and remove from skillet. Melt margarine or butter in skillet, cook sliced onions until golden brown. Return meat to skillet, add remaining ingredients except sour cream. Cover and simmer 2 hours. At serving time, stir in sour cream and heat thoroughly below a boil. Serve over buttered noodles. Yield: 6–8 servings

Baked ham with glazes

For 1 precooked, about 6 pounds.
Yield: 6-8 servings

Apricot glaze:

    2 jars (12 ounces) apricot preserves
    2 tablespoons lime juice
    1½ teaspoons whole cloves
    ½ teaspoon *potpourri liqueur*
    ½ cup *angelica liqueur*

Combine all ingredients in saucepan. Heat well. Brush over ham. Cook 35 minutes at 350°, basting frequently until glaze browns.

Orange glaze:

    1 cup orange marmalade
    ½ cup *orange liqueur*
    1 teaspoon dry mustard

Follow directions for Apricot glaze.

Minted roast leg of lamb

 1 leg of lamb (6 pounds)
 ⅓ cup of Dijon mustard
 2 tablespoons soy sauce
 1 clove garlic, crushed
 1 teaspoon *rosemary liqueur*
 ½ cup *mint liqueur*

Place lamb on a rack in shallow roasting pan. Roast at 325° for 1 hour. Combine remaining ingredients and pour over lamb. Roast an additional 1½ hours, basting often.

Glazed cranberry meatloaf

 2 pounds ground beef
 1 cup herbed bread crumbs
 2 eggs, slightly beaten
 1 small onion, grated
 Salt and pepper to taste

Sauce:
 ½ cup dry red wine
 ½ cup brown sugar
 1 can (1-pound) whole berry cranberry sauce
 ½ teaspoon *cranberry liqueur*
 ¼ teaspoon *allspice liqueur*
 ¼ teaspoon cloves
 1 tablespoon cornstarch

Mix together meatloaf ingredients and shape. Place in greased pan. For sauce, mix together wine and sugar, add cranberry sauce, liqueurs, and cloves. Mix. Spread ¾ of the mixture atop the meatloaf. Bake at 350° for 1 hour. Remove meat to hot platter. Blend together the cornstarch and remaining sauce. Stir into pan drippings and cook until thick. Slice, serve, and pass the sauce. Yield: 4 servings

Steak Diane flambé

    4 thin individual steaks, or 1 sirloin steak 2–3
            pounds, sliced in 1″–2″ slices
    Salt and pepper
    Dry mustard
    5 tablespoons butter
    1 tablespoon Worcestershire sauce
    2 tablespoons parsley or chives
    1 tablespoon lemon juice
    ¼ cup *berry liqueur* warmed

Season meat with salt, pepper, and dry mustard. Pound
with mallet. Melt butter in fry pan, sear steak on both
sides. Remove to warm serving plate. Add remaining
ingredients to pan juices. Light with a match, pour
sauce over steaks.
Yield: 4 servings

Veal scallopine

    1½ pounds veal cutlets, thinly sliced
    ¼ cup flour
    Salt and pepper
    1 tablespoon butter
    1 tablespoon olive oil
    ½ pound sliced mushrooms
    ½ cup sauterne
    ½ cup water
    2 teaspoons *orange liqueur*
    Parsley

Dredge veal in seasoned flour. Heat butter with oil in
heavy skillet. Sauté meat until browned. Add remaining
ingredients except parsley and simmer until tender,
about ½ hour. Garnish with parsley.

Fresh chicken with fruity liqueur basting sauce and mint liqueur spinach

11

Elegant Entrées - Chicken

Cranberry chicken

    2 3-pound fryers, quartered
    Salt and pepper
    1 1-pound can whole berry cranberry sauce
    1 teaspoon *cranberry liqueur*
    1 teaspoon *orange liqueur*
    1 8-ounce bottle French salad dressing

Place chicken in roasting pan and season. Mix cranberry sauce with liqueurs and pour over chicken. Add French dressing. Cover and bake at 350° for 1 hour.
Yield: 4 servings

> Add allspice, sage, rosemary, walnut, raisin, apple, or pineapple liqueur to your favorite poultry stuffing. Substitute ⅓ of the liquid called for with liqueur.

Barbecued ginger chicken

1 roasting chicken, about 4 pounds
Salt and pepper
½ cup soy sauce
¼ cup honey
¾ cup *ginger liqueur*
3 tablespoons lemon juice
½ cup chicken broth

Season chicken inside and out with salt and pepper. Combine remaining ingredients. Brush cavity. Let stand 1 hour. Arrange bird on electric spit. Brush outside. Roast at 350° about 1½ hours until chicken is done, basting often.
Yield: 4–6 servings

Fresh chicken with fruity liqueur basting sauce

4 tablespoons butter or margarine
¼ teaspoon each mace and nutmeg
1 teaspoon salt
1 tablespoon brown sugar
3 medium-sized peaches pitted or ½ can pitted
    Bing cherries puréed in blender or food
    processor
2 tablespoons frozen orange juice concentrate
2 tablespoons lemon juice
4 tablespoons *fruit liqueur—peach, cherry,* or *lemon-lime*
1 frying chicken, cut-up

Melt butter or margarine and add spices, salt, sugar, stirring only until well blended. Mix separately puréed fruit and remaining ingredients. Add to spice mixture; heat again and stir until smooth. Do not boil. Place cut-up frying chicken in pan lined with enough foil so it can be brought over the chicken and folded to close. Broil chicken in pan lined with foil open about 7 inches from heat for 10 minutes or until browned. Brown both sides of chicken. Baste with half the sauce and broil 5 more minutes on each side. Baste with remaining sauce. Close the foil and fold over, allowing only a small opening for steam to escape. Reduce heat to 375° and bake about 30 minutes. Serve with extra fruit warmed.

Yield: 4 servings

Glazed Cornish hens

    2 small Rock Cornish hens
    Brown rice
    2 tablespoons melted butter
    1 small jar currant jelly
    1 teaspoon *orange liqueur*
    1 teaspoon *lemon-lime liqueur*
    1 small can frozen orange juice concentrate
    Salt and pepper

Salt and pepper hens and cavities. Stuff with rice. Brush with melted butter. Bake at 350° for ½ hour. Combine jelly, liqueurs, and orange juice. Spread over hens. Bake an additional 40 minutes, basting with sauce.

Yield: 2 servings

Use the same glaze for chickens and turkeys. Substitute the citrus flavors with other fruit flavors as desired.

12

Elegant Entrées - Fish

Sole angelica

⅔ cup slivered almonds
⅔ cup butter
¼ cup *angelica liqueur*
¼ cup fresh lemon juice
½ teaspoon dill
Freshly ground pepper
2 pounds fillet of sole

Blanch almonds by sautéing in butter in large skillet until toasted lightly. When butter browns, stir in angelica liqueur, lemon juice, dill, and pepper. Add fish. Cover, cook over medium heat 7-10 minutes, or until sole flakes easily with a fork. Baste with sauce often as the fish cooks.

This fish entree is delightful to the eye and palate. Photo courtesy *Cuisine* magazine, Chicago, IL.

Polynesian scallops

> ⁻½ cup oil
> ½ cup soy sauce
> ½ cup *pineapple liqueur*
> ½ teaspoon ginger
> 1 clove garlic, minced
> 1½ pounds scallops

Combine first five ingredients in a bowl. Marinate scallops in this mixture one to two hours. Place scallops on skewers. Broil about 2″ from heat for 5 minutes, turning often and basting with the sauce. Serve at once.

Mix ¼ to ½ teaspoon *lime* or *lemon liqueur* with lemon butter and serve with fish.

A touch of *almond* or *herbed liqueur* brings out a delicious fish flavor.

Serve cold fish with *spice* and *citrus liqueurs* mixed into a cream or butter fish sauce. Salmon, tuna, mahi-mahi, and other fish are excellent served with liqueured sauces. Always add the liqueur with a liquid ingredient or stir it in after mixing all other ingredients. Experiment.

13

Sumptuous Soups

Vegetable beef soup

>   1 cup dried bean soup mix
>   6 cups water
>   6 beef bouillon cubes
>   (6 cups beef soup stock may be substituted for
>   water and bouillon)
>   ½ cup carrots sliced
>   ½ cup peas fresh or frozen
>   2 tablespoons *anise liqueur*

Simmer bean soup mix, water, and bouillon for one hour. Add carrots and fresh peas and simmer for ½ hour. If using frozen peas, add them only during the last five minutes. Add anise liqueur a few minutes before serving. Additional liqueur may be added to individual soup bowls to taste.
Yield: 4-6 servings

Vegetable beef soup with anise liqueur

Curried coconut soup

1⅓ cups flaked coconut
1½ cups milk
1 tablespoon cornstarch
½ teaspoon curry powder
⅛ teaspoon salt
1½ cups chicken broth
1½ teaspoons *coconut liqueur*
Plain yogurt
Toasted coconut

To make coconut milk, blend coconut and milk together in food processor or blender. Strain mixture, reserving as much milk as possible. Discard coconut or add to "Fruitueur's Fantasy." In saucepan, blend cornstarch, curry, and salt. Stir in coconut milk and broth gradually. Add coconut liqueur. Cook and stir until mixture comes to a boil. Serve hot or cold. Garnish with a dollop of yogurt, and coconut.
Yield: 4 servings

Plantation peanut soup

⅛ cup butter or margarine
½ small onion, chopped
1 rib celery, chopped
1½ tablespoons flour
4 cups chicken broth
½ cup peanut butter
2 tablespoons *peanut liqueur*
⅛ teaspoon celery salt
¼ teaspoon salt
½ tablespoon lemon juice
Ground peanuts for garnish

Sauté celery and onion in soup pot. Add flour and mix. Gradually add chicken broth. Cook 35 minutes. Remove from heat. Strain off vegetables and discard. Add peanut butter, liqueur, salts, and lemon juice, stirring until peanut butter dissolves. Serve hot, garnished with ground peanuts.

Yield: 4 servings

Cheese soup

    1 can condensed celery soup
    1 can condensed consomme
    1¼ cups water or milk
    ½ cup grated cheddar or pimiento cheese
    2 tablespoons *caraway liqueur*
    Chopped parsley

Combine and stir soups, water or milk, and cheese over low heat until cheese melts. Do not boil. Add liqueur and chopped parsley just before serving.

Yield: 4 servings

Cold avocado soup

> 2 cans cream of chicken soup
> 1 ripe avocado
> ½ cup heavy cream
> ⅛ teaspoon pepper
> 2 teaspoons *anise liqueur*
> 1 teaspoon chopped chives (garnish)

Pureé soup and avocado in a blender or food processor. Chill. At serving time, stir in cream, pepper, and liqueur. Garnish with chives. If you prefer soup thinner, add a little milk, and stir until desired consistency.
Yield: 2 servings

Serve bottles of various flavored herb liqueurs with beef, vegetable, and chicken soups. Use a dash, or a teaspoon or so, as you would use a condiment.

Cold cherry soup

  16 ounces sour cherries, pitted
  5 cups water
  ½ cup sugar
  3 tablespoons lemon juice
  ½ teaspoon cinnamon
  ½ cup water
  3 tablespoons cornstarch
  ½ teaspoon salt
  1 teaspoon *almond liqueur*
  3 tablespoons *cherry liqueur*
  1 cup sour cream or yogurt

Slightly mash cherries. Combine with 5 cups water, sugar, lemon juice, and cinnamon. Cover and cook slowly for 30 minutes. Dissolve cornstarch with ½ cup water. Add to cherry mixture along with salt and liqueurs. Cook until soup clears and begins to thicken. Serve cold with a dollop of sour cream or yogurt.
Yield: 6 servings

14

Super Salads

Coleslaw

> 1 head cabbage
> 3 carrots
> 1 cup sour cream
> ⅔ cup mayonnaise
> 2½ tablespoons sugar
> 2½ tablespoons vinegar
> 1 tablespoon salt
> 1 teaspoon ground white pepper
> 1 tablespoon *anise liqueur*

Shred cabbage and carrots and mix with remaining ingredients. Chill 2 to 4 hours before serving. Taste. Adjust flavorings.
Yield: 8 servings

Pyramid peach mold and Waldorf salad with cassis liqueur

Creamy peach mold

    1 6-ounce package orange gelatin
    ½ cup hot water
    1 cup hot peach syrup
    1 cup canned peaches, drained
    ½ cup *peach liqueur*
    ½ cup whipping cream (optional)
    Fresh or frozen peach slices for garnish

Dissolve gelatin in hot water and peach syrup; cool. Combine gelatin mixture, canned peaches, and liqueur in blender or food processor. Beat until blended and smooth. Add cream and whip for 2 seconds. Pour into 1-quart mold and chill until firm. Unmold on platter and garnish with peach slices.

Spinach salad flambé

    1½ pounds fresh spinach, stems removed
    ½ pound bacon, diced
    ½ cup wine vinegar
    2 tablespoons Worcestershire sauce
    ¼ cup lemon juice
    ½ cup sugar
    ¼ cup *lemon-lime liqueur*

Wash spinach well, pat dry. Sauté bacon. Add vinegar, Worcestershire sauce, lemon juice, and sugar. When sugar begins to boil, pour over spinach. Add warmed liqueur to pan, light with a match, pour flaming over spinach salad.

> Add liqueurs to the cooled liquids when making gelatin molds. Substitute ⅓ of the liquid called for with liqueur.

Tangerine crab salad

½ pound fresh crabmeat
2–3 fresh Tangeloes, sectioned
¼ cup *tangerine liqueur*
½ cup celery, diced
2 tablespoons onion, chopped
¼ cup Thousand Island salad dressing
Salt to taste
Lettuce

Combine first five ingredients. Mix with Thousand Island dressing, salt to taste. Serve cold on a bed of lettuce.

Waldorf salad

2 cups apples, diced, unpared
1 cup diced celery
½ cup walnut pieces
½ teaspoon *cassis liqueur*
Mayonnaise
Lettuce

Combine first four ingredients. Gradually add enough mayonnaise to bind the mix together. Refrigerate for several hours or overnight. Serve on a bed of lettuce. Yield: 6 servings

Dona's squash, carrot, and apple casserole with orange liqueur

15

Vibrant Vegetables

Dona's squash, carrot, and apple casserole

    2-3 pounds banana squash (or other winter variety)
    3 carrots
    1 apple
    ½ cup brown sugar
    ½ teaspoon nutmeg
    ¼ teaspoon cinnamon
    ½ cup lemon juice
    2 tablespoons margarine
    1 cup raisins
    ¼ cup *orange liqueur* or *apple liqueur*

Cut away the outer skin of squash and remove seeds. Cut into small pieces about ¾ inch and place in large baking dish. Cut carrots, pare and cut apple, add to baking dish. Then, sprinkle with sugar, cinnamon, nutmeg, lemon juice. Dot with butter. Cover and bake at 400° about 1 hour. Add raisins and stir gently. Bake 15-30 minutes or until all squash is soft. Stir in liqueur. Yield: 8-10 servings

Savory Brussels sprouts

> ¾ pound Brussels sprouts
> 1 cup chicken broth
> ¼ stick butter, melted
> 2 teaspoons lemon juice
> 1¼ teaspoons *caraway liqueur*
> ¼ teaspoon salt
> Freshly ground pepper
> 1 tablespoon bread crumbs
> 1 tablespoon butter

Cook sprouts in broth over medium high heat 5 minutes or until barely tender, drain. Mix sprouts with butter, lemon juice, liqueur, salt, and pepper. Place in baking dish, sprinkle with bread crumbs, and dot with butter. Pop into preheated broiler until crumbs are golden.
Yield: 4 servings

Mushrooms au gratin

> 1 pound fresh mushrooms
> 2 tablespoons margarine
> ⅓ cup sour cream
> ¼ teaspoon pepper
> 1 tablespoon flour
> 1 teaspoon *anise liqueur*
> ¼ cup minced parsley
> ½ cup shredded cheddar or Swiss cheese

Slice mushrooms. Cook in butter until brown. Blend sour cream, salt, pepper, flour, and liqueur until smooth. Turn into baking dish. Sprinkle remaining ingredients evenly over top. Bake at 400° for 15 minutes.
Yield: 4-6 servings

Quick and creative vegetables with liqueurs.

Vegetables caraway

Sprinkle cooked cabbage (or broccoli, Brussels sprouts, or cauliflower) with *caraway liqueur.*

Vegetables anisette

Add a dash of *anise liqueur* and give welcome licorice flavor to cooked beets, carrots, celery, or to a cheese sauce for any vegetable.

Minty vegetables

Cook peas, carrots, spinach, or summer squash until tender. Drain, season, add butter, sugar, and a lively dash of *mint liqueur.*

Liqueur-glazed vegetables

Sprinkle cooked carrots, winter squash, or sweet potatoes with butter, sugar, and *apricot liqueur, peach liqueur,* or *pineapple liqueur.* Baste over low heat until glazed. Or broil or bake until brown.

Baked beans à l'orange

A new flavor for baked beans: add one teaspoon per portion of *orange liqueur* before heating!

Spirited broccoli

    1 pound fresh broccoli
    ¼ cup melted butter
    3 tablespoons flour
    ½ teaspoon salt
    ½ teaspoon *allspice liqueur*
    ⅛ teaspoon oregano
    ¼ cup minced parsley
    1 teaspoon *almond liqueur*
    1 teaspoon lemon juice
    ½ teaspoon *lemon-lime liqueur*

Cook broccoli until tender, drain, reserve 1 cup liquid. In saucepan, blend ingredients listed except for lemon juice and lemon-lime liqueur. Slowly add reserved liquid and stir until thickened and smooth. Add lemon flavorings.
Yield: 4–6 servings

"House special" yam casserole

  6 large yams or sweet potatoes
  Butter
  1 tablespoon brown sugar
  ¼ cup orange juice
  ¼ cup *tangerine* or *orange* or *pineapple liqueur*
  1 teaspoon *apricot liqueur*
  ½ teaspoon cinnamon
  ¼ teaspoon nutmeg
  Sliced oranges, tangerine or pineapple and
    marshmallows for garnish

Cook and mash potatoes. Add remaining ingredients
except for garnish. Adjust spices. Garnish with tangerine, pineapple, or orange slices and marshmallows. Bake
at 350° for 30 minutes.
Yield: 6-8 servings

Richard's famous omelette

16

Exotic Eggs and Cheeses

Richard's famous omelette

4 medium-sized mushrooms, diced
½ green pepper, diced
3 tablespoons butter
4 eggs
1 tablespoon *caraway liqueur*
Scant ¼ teaspoon salt
4 drops Tabasco sauce
½ teaspoon basil
Freshly ground pepper
6 slices Longhorn Colby cheese
1 tablespoon Parmesan/Romano cheese

Lightly sauté mushrooms and green peppers in butter. Mix eggs, caraway liqueur, salt, and Tabasco in bowl with wire whip. Add to vegetables in skillet. Keep flame *very low*. Season with dill and pepper. Add Colby cheese, sprinkle with Parmesan/Romano cheese. Cook *very slowly* for 8 minutes.
Yield: 2 servings

Eggs Benedict

8 slices cooked ham
8 eggs
8 slices English Muffins
Black olives (optional)

Hollandaise sauce:

4 egg yolks
½ cup butter or margarine, melted
½ cup boiling water
1½ tablespoons lemon juice
2 tablespoons *anise liqueur*
¼ teaspoon salt
Dash cayenne

To make Hollandaise sauce:
Beat egg yolks slightly in top of double boiler. Stir in butter, gradually add water, beating constantly. Cook, stirring over hot water in double boiler just until thickened. Remove top of double boiler. Gradually stir remaining ingredients into mixture. Cover, keep warm.

Broil ham until lightly browned. Keep warm. Poach eggs, drain. Toast muffins. On each plate, place a whole, opened muffin. Top with ham. Place eggs atop ham.

Spoon Hollandaise over eggs. Garnish with black olives.

Yield: 4 servings

Baked apple pancake

    4 tart apples, peeled, sliced thin
    3 tablespoons *lemon liqueur*
    2 tablespoons butter
    1 teaspoon salt
    1 cup milk
    1 cup flour
    6 eggs, beaten
    Cinnamon-sugar
    3 tablespoons *orange liqueur*

Mix apples with lemon liqueur. Melt butter in skillet, sauté apples until glazed. In a bowl, mix salt, milk, flour, and eggs, beating constantly. Pour batter over apples and bake in a pre-heated 450° oven for 20 minutes. Reduce heat to 350° and bake an additional 10 minutes until crisp and brown. Remove from oven, sprinkle with cinnamon-sugar. Pour orange liqueur over all, ignite, and flame.
Yield: 6-8 servings

Cheese fondue

    1 pound Swiss cheese
    1 pound Edam cheese
    2 tablespoons flour
    2 cloves garlic
    1½ cups white wine
    Salt and pepper
    2 tablespoons *cherry liqueur*
    French bread, cut in bite-sized chunks

Grate cheese, toss with flour. Rub fondue pan with garlic cloves. Pour in wine, heat until it bubbles. Gradually add small amounts of cheese. Stir constantly. Add salt and pepper to taste. Stir for an additional 8 minutes, or until mixture reaches a good consistency for coating dipped bread. Stir in liqueur just before serving.
Yield: 8 servings

Cranberry Welsh rarebit

    2 tablespoons butter
    1 pound sharp cheddar cheese, grated
    ⅓ cup *cranberry liqueur*
    1 egg
    ½ teaspoon salt

Heat butter in saucepan. Add cheese and liqueur. Cook over low heat, stirring often until cheese melts. Remove from heat. Beat egg with salt, gradually add to cheese mixture, stirring until well mixed. Heat through, stirring, about 5 minutes. Serve over toast.
Yield: 4-6 servings

17

Bravo Breads, Muffins, Toast

French toast à l'orange

4 eggs
¾ cup milk
¼ cup *orange liqueur*
1 tablespoon sugar
½ teaspoon vanilla
¼ teaspoon salt
8 slices thick-sliced bread
2 tablespoons margarine or butter
Cinnamon

Combine eggs with milk, orange liqueur, sugar, vanilla, and salt. Beat well. Dip bread in mixture, turn, coat well. Arrange in a single layer in baking pan. Cover and refrigerate overnight. Heat butter in large skillet. Sauté bread on both sides until golden brown. Sprinkle with cinnamon.
Yield: 4 servings

French toast à l'orange

Pumpkin bread
(Use 3 Loaf Pans)

> 3½ cups flour
> 2 teaspoons baking soda
> 1½ teaspoons salt
> 1 teaspoon cinnamon
> 1 teaspoon nutmeg
> 3 cups sugar
> 1 cup oil
> 4 eggs
> ¼ cup *walnut liqueur*
> ½ cup water
> 1 1-pound can pumpkin
> 2 cups chopped walnuts

Sift all dry ingredients together in a mixing bowl. Make a well in the middle, add all ingredients except nuts. Blend well, add nuts. Pour into 3 greased and floured loaf pans. Bake at 350° for 1 hour. Cool in pans for 10 minutes, turn out, and finish cooling on a rack.

Popovers

> 1 cup sifted all-purpose flour
> ½ teaspoon salt
> 1 cup milk
> 2 eggs
> 1 teaspoon *lemon-lime, pineapple, orange,* or *tangerine liqueur*
> Vegetable oil

Preheat oven to 425°. Blend all ingredients except oil together just until smooth. *Do not overblend.* Oil 8 custard cups or a large muffin tin. Fill each cup ½ to ⅔ full. Bake until golden and popped, about 25 minutes. Yield: 8 servings

When adding a tablespoon of liqueur into the liquid portion of bread and muffin packaged mixes, reduce the initial liquid by about ⅓ and substitute the liqueur. Use fruit, nut, coffee, vanilla, and similar flavored liqueurs.

Fresh blueberry muffins

1 cup fresh blueberries
¼ cup *cassis* or *apple* or *banana liqueur*
2 cups flour
¼ cup butter
¼ cup sugar
1 egg, beaten
4 teaspoons baking powder
½ teaspoon salt
¾ cup milk

Mix blueberries with liqueur, then coat with ¼ cup flour. Cream butter and sugar and add egg. Sift dry ingredients with remaining flour. Stir in berries and milk. Bake in greased muffin pans for 25 minutes at 425°.
Yield: 1 dozen

Fill chocolates and fruits with flavored liqueurs using a grown-up hypodermic needle.

18

Creative Candies and Confections

Liqueured fruits

Use a grown-up hypodermic needle in the kitchen. Fill the tube with your favorite liqueur and "vaccinate" chocolate candy, fresh strawberries, grapes, kumquats, and other small fruits with any variety of flavors. Also use it to fill chocolates and cupcakes, for basting foods, and wherever you can put it to work creatively. Available in photo supply and kitchen stores.

Coffee-chocolate balls

    1 8½-ounce package chocolate wafers, crushed
    1 cup chopped pecans
    ½ cup light corn syrup
    ¼ cup *coffee liqueur*
    1 cup confectioners' sugar

Combine all ingredients, except confectioners' sugar. Mix well. Shape teaspoons of mixture into small balls. Let stand 15 minutes. Roll in confectioners' sugar.

English toffee

    1¾ cups sugar
    ⅛ teaspoon cream of tartar
    1 cup cream
    ½ cup butter
    1 teaspoon *cherry liqueur*

Combine sugar and cream of tartar in a deep saucepan. Add cream, boil for 3 minutes, always stirring with wooden spoon. Add butter, boil to soft-crack stage, 290°, constantly stirring. Add liqueur. Pour into buttered pan. Cut into squares while warm.

Holiday fruit balls

    ½ cup chopped walnuts
    1½ cups dried apricots, chopped
    2 cups flaked coconut
    ⅔ cup sweetened condensed milk
    1 teaspoon *coconut liqueur*
    Confectioners' sugar

Combine nuts, apricots, and coconut in mixing bowl. Refrigerate until firm. Shape into 1″ balls and roll in sugar. Refrigerate.

Candied citrus peel

Use the peels from oranges, lemons, and limes for candy when you use the fruits for liqueurs.

> 2 cups any citrus peel
> 1½ cups cold water

Cut peels into thin strips; scrape away any of the white part or the pulp. Place in heavy pan with enough water to cover. Bring slowly to boil and simmer 15 minutes. Drain. Repeat this process 3 times with fresh cold water each time. Rind should be soft when pierced with a toothpick; if not, continue simmering the last time until the rind is soft. Drain thoroughly.

For each cup of peels, make a syrup of:

> ¼ cup water
> ½ cup sugar
> 1 tablespoon *orange liqueur* or *apricot liqueur*

Combine sugar and water and heat until sugar dissolves. Add liqueur. Bring to a boil. Add peel and cook over low heat until syrup is absorbed and peel has candied appearance. Remove a few peels at a time, drip off any excess syrup and roll peels in powdered sugar. Spread on racks to dry. They are ready for eating or may be dipped in chocolate coating. Refer to a candy making book for recipe and procedures for chocolate coating.

19

Dynamic Desserts

Bananas flambé

½ cup brown sugar
¼ cup butter
4 ripe bananas, quartered
Dash cinnamon
1 tablespoon lemon juice
½ cup light rum
¼ cup *banana* or *orange* or *almond liqueur*
½ cup vanilla ice cream

Melt brown sugar and butter in skillet. Add bananas and
sauté until soft, don't overcook. Sprinkle cinnamon and
lemon juice over bananas. Heat rum and liqueur in
saucepan, without stirring sauce; pour over bananas.
Ignite liqueur and keep spooning sauce over the bananas
until flame dies. Spoon bananas and sauce over ice
cream; serve now!

Chocolate mint walnut mousse. Photo courtesy Diamond Walnut Growers, Inc., Stockton, CA

Citrus rice pudding

½ cup dark raisins
½ cup *citrus liqueur*
1 quart milk
¾ cup sugar
½ cup uncooked long-grain rice
2 teaspoons grated orange peel
1 teaspoon grated lemon peel
2 teaspoons vanilla
2-3 drops orange extract
1½ cups whipping cream, whipped
6-8 orange segments

Soak raisins in liqueur; reserve. Combine milk, sugar, rice, orange peel and lemon peel in medium-size saucepan. Heat to boiling; reduce heat. Simmer covered, stir occasionally, until most of the milk is absorbed, 45-60 minutes. Stir in raisins with liqueur, vanilla and orange extract during last 10 minutes of cooking. Cool. Fold whipped cream into pudding. Spoon into serving bowl; garnish with orange segments.

Chocolate sauce flambé

1 6-ounce package semi-sweet chocolate pieces
1 tablespoon butter
¼ cup light corn syrup
¼ cup milk
¼ cup *coffee liqueur*
Ice cream

Melt chocolate and butter in top of double boiler over hot water. Slowly stir in syrup and milk; beat until smooth. In a small saucepan warm liqueur. Ignite. Pour flaming liqueur into chocolate mixture. When flame subsides, stir well and spoon over ice cream.

Creative chocolate mousse

Add excitement to chocolate mousse with a variety of liqueurs. The ingredients and preparation for each of the following are similar but the liqueurs make the difference.

Tangerine chocolate mousse

>   1 6-ounce package semi-sweet chocolate bits
>   5 eggs separated
>   ¼ cup *tangerine liqueur*
>   1 teaspoon grated orange peel
>   2 tablespoons sugar
>   1 cup heavy cream, whipped

Melt chocolate over low heat. Beat egg yolks until thick, add and beat into melted chocolate. Stir in tangerine liqueur and orange rind. Beat egg whites until soft peaks form. Slowly add sugar, beating until stiff. Fold whites into chocolate mixture, then fold in whipped cream. Spoon into individual serving dishes or into a 6-cup mold and chill several hours, overnight, or until set.

Mocha mousse

Substitute tangerine liqueur and orange peel with ¼ cup *coffee liqueur*.

Chocolate cherry mousse

Substitute ¼ cup coffee liqueur with ¼ cup *cherry liqueur*.

Chocolate mint walnut mousse

Substitute ¼ cup above liqueur with ¼ cup *mint liqueur* and ½ cup chopped walnuts.

Chocolate fondue

½ cup heavy cream
1 12-ounce Swiss milk chocolate bar
2 tablespoons *orange liqueur*
Assorted fresh fruits (banana slices, strawberries,
    seedless grapes, melon chunks, pineapple
    chunks, orange segments)
Bite-sized pieces of pound cake

Combine whipping cream and chocolate in saucepan over low heat, stirring until chocolate melts and mixture is smooth. Remove from heat; stir in liqueur. Pour into fondue pot. To serve, spear fruits and cake and dip into chocolate.
Yield: 8 servings

Harvey Wallbanger cake

1 package orange cake mix
1 package instant vanilla pudding
½ cup oil
¾ cup orange juice
4 eggs
¼ cup vodka
¼ cup *angelica liqueur*

Frosting:
1 cup confectioner's sugar
1½ tablespoons orange juice
1½ tablespoons vodka
1½ tablespoons *angelica liqueur*

Combine all cake ingredients, beat until smooth. Pour into greased and floured 10″ Bundt™ pan or angel food pan. Bake at 350° for 50 minutes. Combine frosting ingredients and drizzle over warm cake.

Frozen crèmes

> 1 cup heavy cream
> ¼ cup *coffee, almond, chocolate, pistachio,* or *fruit liqueur*
> 1 pint vanilla ice cream, well softened
> ⅓ cup finely chopped, toasted almonds

Beat cream until stiff peaks form. Combine cream, ice cream, and liqueur. Pour into lined muffin tins. Sprinkle with almonds and freeze until firm.
Yield: 6 servings

Easy snowballs

> 1 package vanilla wafers
> Strawberry jam
> Sliced bananas
> 1 cup heavy cream
> 1 teaspoon vanilla
> 2 tablespoons *banana liqueur*
> ½ cup flaked coconut

Make sandwiches of two vanilla wafers with jam and a slice of banana between. Whip cream, add vanilla, and liqueur. Roll sandwiches in whipped cream and place on waxed paper. Drizzle with flaked coconut.

Mix 2–3 teaspoons of any liqueur into whipped cream or non-dairy whipped topping and use over desserts or as dips for fresh fruit.

Baked peaches in orange liqueur

> 2 pounds fresh peaches
> ¼ cup butter
> 1 cup sugar
> ½ cup *orange liqueur*
> ¼ cup lemon juice
> ½ cup slivered almonds
> Whipped cream or vanilla ice cream for topping

Cut peaches in half; pit. Arrange peaches in greased baking dish, cut side up. Cream together butter and sugar; stir in liqueur and lemon juice. Spoon mixture over peaches, filling the cavities. Sprinkle with almonds. Bake at 375° for 35-40 minutes. Baste with juices. Serve warm with dollop of whipped cream or vanilla ice cream if desired.

Yogurt pie

> 1 9″ graham cracker pie crust or frozen deep dish
>   pie crust
> 2 8-ounce containers lemon yogurt
> 1 8-ounce container non-dairy whipped topping
> 1 teaspoon *coconut liqueur*
> ⅓ cup "Fruitueur's Fantasy" (page 23)

Combine yogurt, topping, and liqueur. Spread "Fruitueur's Fantasy" on bottom of pie shell, and add yogurt mixture. Refrigerate 3-4 hours. Dust with grated lemon peel.

Optional combinations: try vanilla and honey yogurt with *papaya liqueur*. Blackberry yogurt with *cassis*. Use your imagination—anything goes!

California walnut eggnog cake

1 10″ sponge cake, prepared from a mix or your
own recipe

Filling:
¾ cup butter
3 cups powdered sugar
5 egg yolks
4 ounces *egg liqueur*
⅓ cup brandy
1½ teaspoons vanilla
¼ teaspoon nutmeg
1 cup walnuts, chopped fine
1 pint whipping cream
2 teaspoons *walnut liqueur*
2 tablespoons walnut halves for garnish
Red or green maraschino cherries for garnish

Bake sponge cake and let cool. To prepare filling, cream
butter and sugar until light and fluffy. Beat in egg yolks,
one at a time. Mix egg liqueur and brandy and add to
egg yolks. Add vanilla, nutmeg, and walnuts. Slice cake
into four layers and spread filling between each. Frost
top and sides with whipped cream, sweetened and
flavored with walnut liqueur to taste. Garnish with
walnut halves and cherries. Dust with nutmeg. Chill
one hour.
Yield: 12 servings

Add the "Fruitueur's Fantasy" (page 23) on bottoms of pie shells, as layers in parfait glasses, on
the bottoms of puddings, and over ice cream.

Almond crescents

½ cup butter
½ cup shortening
⅓ cup sugar
1 tablespoon *almond liqueur*
1 teaspoon vanilla
2 cups flour
½ cup chopped almonds
Confectioners' sugar

Cream butter and shortening together until fluffy. Add sugar. Add liqueur and vanilla, then flour and nuts. Chill 3–4 hours. Form dough in long rolls 1½" across. Cut in 3" lengths and shape into crescents. Bake on an ungreased cookie sheet at 325° for 15 minutes. Do not brown. Cool slightly, then dip in confectioners' sugar. Yield: 2 dozen

Cream cheese filled brownies

Your favorite brownie recipe or mix
Filling:
1 8-ounce package cream cheese
⅓ cup sugar
1 egg
1 teaspoon *almond liqueur*

Filling: allow cream cheese to soften, combine with sugar, egg, and liqueur. Mix well. Prepare brownie recipe. Pour ½ brownie batter into a greased 8" square pan. Spread with cream cheese mixture and pour remaining chocolate batter on top. Bake at 350° for 45 minutes. Cool.

California walnut eggnog cake. Photo courtesy Diamond Walnut Growers, Inc., Stockton, CA.

Pistachio-mint pudding parfait

 4 tablespoons "Fruitueur's Fantasy" (page 23)
 1 package instant pistachio pudding (3¾ oz.)
 2 cups cold milk
 8 tablespoons *black walnut liqueur*
 ½ pint chocolate mint ice cream
 Non-dairy topping or whipped cream

Spoon one tablespoon "Fruitueur's Fantasy" into each of 4 parfait glasses. Prepare pistachio pudding mix with milk and divide equally into the four glasses. Refrigerate until set. Gently place two tablespoons liqueur on top of pudding in each glass. Spoon in ice cream above rim of glass. Garnish with topping or whipped cream. Yield: 4 servings

Frozen grasshopper pie

Crust:

    24 chocolate Oreo or Hydrox cookies, finely
        crushed
    ¼ cup melted butter

Filling:

    ¼ cup *mint liqueur*
    ¼ cup *chocolate liqueur*
    1 7-ounce jar marshmallow crème
    2 cups heavy cream, whipped
    Pinch of green food coloring

Combine cookie crumbs with butter. Reserve ½ cup for topping. Press crumbs into bottom of 9″ pie plate. Bake in 400° oven for 5 minutes. Cool. For filling, gradually blend liqueurs into marshmallow creme. Fold whipped cream into marshmallow mixture. Add food coloring and pour into crumb-lined pan. Sprinkle reserved crumbs around edge and in center of pie. Freeze several hours until firm.

Yield: 8–10 servings

Ice cream cake supreme

Be creative! Your ideas will make this cake a hit. Use *apricot* or *almond liqueur* with pistachio and strawberry ice cream. Or *orange liqueur* with peach and black raspberry ice cream. Try *coconut liqueur* with pineapple and vanilla. The choices are unlimited.

    1 angel food cake prepared from a mix or your
        own recipe
    ½ cup liqueur
    2 1-pint containers of ice cream
    2 cups heavy cream

With a sharp, serrated knife, carefully cut cake into three layers. Sprinkle layers with 6 tablespoons of liqueur. Spread bottom layer with one flavor of ice cream. Top with second layer of cake and other flavor of ice cream. Add third cake layer. Wrap in plastic wrap and place in freezer. In a bowl, mix heavy cream and remaining liqueur and beat until thick. Frost sides and top of cake with cream. Garnish with chocolate shavings or finely chopped nuts if desired. Freeze cake until ready to use.

Crêpes

Basic crêpe recipe:

> 1 cup sifted flour
> 1 teaspoon salt
> 2 tablespoons sugar
> 3 eggs, beaten
> 2 cups milk
> 1 tablespoon melted butter
> 1 teaspoon *fruit* or *nut liqueur*

Add sifted ingredients to eggs and milk. Beat well and add butter. Drop batter by spoonfuls onto hot, well greased 4″ skillet until bottom is thinly covered. Bake until bubbly and brown on underside. Turn and brown.

Ice cream liqueur filling:

Fill crêpes with any flavor ice cream topped with liqueur. Try chocolate ice cream topped with 2 tablespoons *coffee* or *mint liqueur*. Garnish with chocolate shavings.

Peach-filled crêpes with peach liqueur. Photo courtesy National Peach Council

Strawberry crêpes Romanoff:

    2 pints fresh strawberries
    ⅓ cup *orange liqueur*
    1 cup confectioners' sugar
    3 tablespoons butter
    1 cup heavy cream, whipped

Crush 1 cup berries for sauce. Combine remaining strawberries with liqueur and confectioners' sugar. Drain berries, reserve liquid, arrange on crêpes, and roll up. Melt butter in large skillet. Add crêpes. Top with drained liquid. Cover and cook on low heat for 10 minutes. Combine crushed strawberries with whipped cream and serve over crêpes.

Fresh peach filling:

> 3 cups fresh peach purée (about 4 large peaches)
> 2 teaspoons ascorbic acid
> 3 tablespoons cornstarch
> 1 cup brown sugar
> ⅛ teaspoon salt
> 3 tablespoons butter
> 2 teaspoons *almond liqueur*
> 2 cups large diced fresh peaches
> Sour cream or whipping cream, optional

Mix peach purée, ascorbic acid, cornstarch, brown sugar, and salt together in saucepan. Place over medium heat and cook until thick, stirring constantly. Add butter and mix until melted. Add liqueur and fresh peaches. Use as filling for dessert crêpes. If desired, each crêpe can be topped with a dollop of sour cream or sweetened whipped cream.
Yield: 20 crêpes

20

Colossal Coffees and Teas

Café brûlot

    1½ ounces *coffee liqueur*
    1 ounce cognac
    1½ ounces *anise liqueur*
    3 lumps sugar
    Strips of lemon peel (½ lemon)
    Strips of orange peel (⅛ orange)
    4 pieces of cinnamon stick (1″ size)
    4 whole cloves
    2 cups of HOT black coffee

In a chafing dish combine the liqueurs and cognac, sugar, fruit peel, cinnamon, and cloves. Stir gently with ladle as this is warming. Ignite. While flaming, slowly add hot coffee. Ladle into demi-tasse cups.

Use your imagination to create your own special mix.

Cappuccino

> 4 cups strong coffee
> 2 cups milk
> 2 jiggers brandy
> 1 jigger *chocolate liqueur*
> 1½ teaspoons cocoa
> 1½ teaspoons sugar
> 4 cinnamon sticks
> Whipped cream

In saucepan, combine coffee, milk, brandy, and liqueur. Mix cocoa and sugar; add to coffee mixture. Heat just until boiling. Pour into mugs. Add cinnamon stick to each mug; top with whipped cream.
NOTE: 1 jigger = 1½ ounces.
Yield: 4 servings

Cranberry tea cooler

> 2 cups cold water
> 4 tea bags
> ½ cup sugar
> ½ teaspoon *allspice liqueur*
> 3 whole cloves
> 2 cups cranberry juice
> ¼ cup lemon juice
> ½ teaspoon *lemon-lime liqueur*
> 1 teaspoon *cranberry liqueur*
> 1 14-ounce bottle club soda

Boil water. Remove from heat; add tea bags, sugar, allspice liqueur, and cloves. Stir well. Cover; let steep for 5 minutes. Strain into large pitcher; cool. Add cranberry juice, lemon juice, and liqueurs. Chill. At serving time, add soda and pour into glasses. Garnish with citrus slices.

Mocha java

Flavor each cup of hot strong coffee with *coffee liqueur*. Add a cinnamon stick for stirring. Top with whipped cream and grated chocolate.

Café après ski

To each cup of hot strong coffee add 1½ ounces of *orange liqueur*. Finish with whipped cream and a dusting of grated orange peel.

Chocolate mint coffee

Add ½ jigger *mint liqueur* to ½ jigger *chocolate liqueur*. Pour into cup. Add hot strong coffee, stir, and top with whipped cream and crushed peppermint.

Almond coffee

Combine 1 ounce of *almond liqueur* to each cup of hot coffee. Top with whipped cream and chopped almonds.

Spiced tea

Orange, tangerine, lemon-lime, cinnamon, ginger, and *anise liqueur* can be added to tea for great flavorings. Try a cinnamon stick for stirring the fruit liqueur into the brewed tea.

Espresso supreme

To each demi-tasse cup of espresso, add one of the following liqueurs: *anise liqueur, mint liqueur, orange liqueur,* or *coffee liqueur*.

Appendix

Following are some convenient equivalents. Also see Chapter 2, page 21.

U. S. liquid measure volume equivalents

A pinch =	Less than ⅛ teaspoon
60 drops =	1 teaspoon
1 teaspoon =	⅓ tablespoon
1 tablespoon =	3 teaspoons or ½ ounce
2 tablespoons =	1 fluid ounce
4 tablespoons =	¼ cup
5⅓ tablespoons =	⅓ cup
8 tablespoons =	½ cup or 4 ounces
16 tablespoons =	1 cup or 8 ounces
1 cup =	½ pint or 8 fluid ounces
2 cups =	1 pint
4 cups =	32 ounces or 1 quart
1 pint liquid =	16 ounces
1 quart liquid =	2 pints or 32 ounces
1 gallon liquid =	4 quarts
⅕ gallon or ⅘ quart =	25.6 ounces

U.S. dry measure equivalents

Dry measure pints and quarts are about ⅙ larger than liquid measure pints and quarts. Dry measure is used for large quantities of raw fruits.

```
1 quart  =   2 pints
8 quarts =   1 peck
4 pecks  =   1 bushel
```

Weight or avoirdupois equivalents

```
1 ounce  =   16 drams
1 pound  =   16 ounces
1 kilo   =   2.20 pounds
```

U.S. and British measure equivalents

Although many British units of measurement have the same name as those in the U.S., they are not all identical. Generally weights are equivalent, but volumes are not.

U.S.

A standard measuring cup or U.S. gill is:

8 ounces = 16 tablespoons = 48 teaspoons

British

The standard measuring cup or Imperial gill is:

10 oz. = 20 U.S. tablespoons = 60 U.S. teaspoons

Liquid measure volume equivalents

1¼ U.S. teaspoons =	1 English *teaspoon*
1¼ U.S. tablespoon =	1 English *tablespoon*
1 U.S. gill =	⅚ English *teacup*
2 U.S. gills =	⅚ English *breakfast* cup
1 U.S. cup =	⅚ English *breakfast* cup
1 U.S. gill =	⅚ English *Imperial* gill
1 U.S. pint =	⅚ English *Imperial* pint
1 U.S. quart =	⅚ English *Imperial* quart
1 U.S. gallon =	⅚ English *Imperial* gallon

U.S. liquid and volume measures and metric equivalents

1 teaspoon =	5 milliliters
1 tablespoon =	15 milliliters
1 ounce =	29.5 milliliters
1 cup (8 ounces) =	237 milliliters
1 pint (16 ounces) =	473 milliliters
⅕ gallon or "fifth" =	¾ liter
1 quart =	.946 liter
½ gallon =	1.9 liters
1 gallon =	3.78 liters

U.S. weight measures and metric equivalents

1 ounce (avoirdupois) =	28.35 grams
¼ pound =	113.4 grams
½ pound =	226.8 grams
1 pound =	454 grams
5 pounds =	2.27 kilograms

Volume and weight equivalents that apply to liqueur making

Almonds—		
unblanched whole	1 cup =	6 ounces
unblanched ground	2⅔ cup =	1 pound
blanched whole	1 cup =	5⅓ ounces
Apples—		
pared/sliced	1 cup =	4 ounces
pared/sliced	3 cups =	1 pound unpared
Bananas—		
unpeeled	3-4 medium =	1 pound
Cocoa	4 cups =	1 pound
Coconut—		
fine grated	3½ ounces =	1 cup
shredded	5 cups =	1 pound
Dates—		
pitted	2½ cups =	1 pound
Herbs—		
dried	⅓ to ½ teaspoon =	1 tablespoon fresh
Lemon rind—		
grated	1 whole =	2 teaspoons
Peanuts—		
shelled	1 pound =	2¼ cup
Pear—		
fresh average	2½ in. diam. =	6 ounces
Pineapple—		
average diced fresh	1 cup =	5 ounces
Plum—		
fresh	2 in. diam. =	2 ounces
Raisins—		
seeded whole	3¼ cups =	1 pound
seedless whole	2¾ cups =	1 pound
Sugar		
granulated	1 cup =	8 ounces
confectioners'	1 cup =	4½ ounces
brown	1 cup =	6 ounces
honey	1 cup =	12 ounces

Walnuts—		
shelled	3½ cups =	1 pound
Water	2 cups =	1 pound

CALORIE CHART

The number of calories per ounce in any given liqueur will vary depending upon the amount of sweetener added and the proof of the base alcohol. The following may help you determine some caloric equivalents. Usually one drinks a lesser amount of liqueurs than of liquors and wines.

Beverage	*Calories per ounce*
Beer	14
Benedictine	110
Bourbon	73
Brandy	75
Green Chartreuse	100
Yellow Chartreuse	125
Crème de menthe	104
Gin	70
Martini (dry) and most mixed cocktails	60
Scotch	73
Wines—	
dry	20 to 30
sweet	40 to 50
Vermouth, dry	25
Vermouth, sweet	44
Vodka	80
Grape juice	10
Grapefruit juice (unsweetened)	7
Quinine water	11
Orange juice	14
Tomato juice	16

SUPPLY SOURCES

The following suppliers will send a price list and/or a catalog. Send a postcard with your inquiry.

Bay Colony Spice Company, Inc. 14 Hayward Street P.O. Box 237 Quincy, Massachusetts 02171	Herbs and Spices
Cuisine Marketplace 133 B West De La Guerra Santa Barbara, California 93101	500 Herbs and Spices
Watkins Products, Inc. Department 7K 150 Liberty Street Winona, Minnesota 55987	Herbs, Spices, and Extracts
Wine-Art of San Diego 460 Fletcher Parkway El Cajon, California 92020	All Noirot Extracts and Some Herbs
The Wine Factory 2761 Teagarden Street San Leandro, California 94577	Noirot Extracts, Cordials, Malts, Extracts
Wine-Maker's Haven 105 North York Road Hatboro, Pennsylvania 19040	Liqueur Making Items, Noirot Extracts

Selected Bibliography

We have found the following books most helpful. Several have only a short chapter or two on liqueurs specifically, but enough to warrant looking through them for background, recipes, and so forth. You will find scores more books available under Liquors, Wines, and Spirits. Watch for recipes in magazines and newspapers.

Many commercial liqueur companies offer booklets with recipes using their products. Often these are available for the asking. Send a postcard requesting them. Occasionally, a small charge is requested to cover the cost of postage and handling. Observe the offers in advertisements for vodka, brandy, and a variety of brand name liqueurs.

Bairachi-Levy, Juliette de. *Common Herbs for Natural Health.* New York, New York: Schocken, 1974.

Balzer, R. L. *Balzer's Book of Wine and Spirits.* Los Angeles, California: Ward Ritchie Press, 1973.

Barbour, Beverly. *Cooking with Spirits.* San Francisco, California: 101 Productions, 1976.

Bennett, H. *The Chemical Formulary.* New York, New York and London, England: Chemical Publishing Company, 1933-1951.

Cocconi, Emilio. *Liqueurs for all Seasons.* Milan, Italy: Fratelli Fabbri, 1974. Wilton, Connecticut: Lyceum Books, Inc., 1975.

Consumer Guide Magazine, Ed. *The Joy of Making Your Own.* Skokie, Illinois: Publications International, Ltd., 1976.

Consumer Union, Ed. *Consumer Union: Report on Wines and Spirits.* Mt. Vernon, New York, 1972.

Farrell, John P. *Making Cordials and Liqueurs at Home.* New York, New York: Harper and Row, Publishers, Inc., 1974.

Fisher, M. F. K. and Eds., Time-Life Books. *The Cooking of Provincial France.* New York, New York: Time-Life Books, 1968.

Fisher, Mary I. *Liqueurs: A Dictionary and Survey.* London, SW1 England: Maurice Meyer, Ltd., 1951.

Fowles, Gerry. *Straight-Forward Liqueur Making.* Woodley, Reading, England: G. Fowles, 1971.

Fox, Helen M. *Gardening with Herbs for Fragrance and Flavor.* New York, New York: Dover Publications, 1972.

Gavin-Jobson, Eds. *The Liquor Handbook.* New York, New York: Gavin-Jobson Associates, Inc., 1976.

Gould, Alec, Ed. *Wines and Spirits of the World.* Chicago, Illinois: Follett Publishing Company, 1972.

Grossman, H. J. *Grossman's Guide to Wines, Spirits and Beers.* New York, New York: Charles Scribner's Sons, 1974.

Hallgarten, Peter. *Liqueurs.* London, England: Wine and Spirit Publications, Ltd., 1967.

Hannum, Hurst and Robert S. Blumberg. *Brandies and Liqueurs of the World.* Garden City, New York: Doubleday and Company, Inc., 1976.

Harrop, Renny, Ed. *Basic Home Preserving.* London, England: Marshall Cavendish Publications, Ltd., 1977.

Johnson, Hugh. *The World Atlas of Wines.* New York, New York: Simon and Schuster, 1971.

Lust, John, Ed. *The Herb Book.* New York, New York: Bantam Publishers, 1974.

Mario, Thomas. *Playboy's Wine and Spirits Cookbook.* Chicago, Illinois: Playboy Press, 1974.

Montagne, Prosper. *Larousse Gastronomique.* New York, New York: Crown Publishers, Inc., 1961.

Rae, Sharon and Gene Paul. *Making Your Own Liqueurs.* Sioux Falls, South Dakota: Raegene Associates, 1974.

Richardson, Collette, Ed. *House and Garden's Drink Guide.* New York, New York: Simon and Schuster, 1973.

Rombauer, Irma S. and Marion Rombauer Becker. *Joy of Cooking Volumes 1 and 2.* New York, New York: New American Library, Inc., 1974.

Rosengarten, Frederick. *Book of Spices.* New York, New York: Pyramid Publications, 1973

Sphere Magazine, Ed. *Herbs, Spices and Essential Oils.* Chicago, Illinois: Sphere Magazine, 1977.

Stone, Jennifer. *Cheap and Easy Cooking with Wines, Liquors, and Liqueurs.* Garden City, New York: Doubleday and Company, Inc., 1974.

Tighe, Eileen, Ed. *Woman's Day Encyclopedia of Cookery Volume 7.* New York, New York: Fawcett Publications, 1966.

Tritton, S. M. *Spirits, Aperitifs and Liqueurs: Their Production.* London, England: Faber and Faber, 1975.

General Index

Key to Index:

DR = Drink Recipe
FR = Food Recipe
LR = Liqueur Recipe
 * = Refers to pages 33 to 35 for basic liqueur flavor
   listing.

See Food and Drink Index for specific recipes. The food
and drink recipe references in the General Index will
help you locate a recipe for a liqueur you may have on
your shelf and wish to use.

Food and Drink Recipe Index

Notes

Notes

Notes